Kenneth E. Behring

Road to Purpose

Dedication

This book is dedicated to all of the people in the world struggling with immobility. Thank you for helping me find my purpose.

Acknowledgments

This book would not have been possible without the help of friends, family members, colleagues at the Wheelchair Foundation and Blackhawk Museum and our philanthropic partners. Many of the stories in the book came from the reports of volunteers and distribution team members who have traveled the world to bring hope, dignity and mobility to thousands of people.

I'd like to thank my editorial team for whipping my manuscript into shape: Peter Barnes, Bill Nixon, Karen Kraft, Meredith Eder and Ernie Anastos.

I'd also like to thank my foundation associates and business colleagues who helped make sure the facts and my recollections were accurate: Steve Beinke, Don Williams, Annette Vineyard, Charli Butterfield, Chris Lewis, Matt Montague, Cheryl Barnes, Jing Sun and Joel Hodge. Thanks to Ling Yan in our Shanghai office for her contributions to my section on our work in China. Special thanks to my son, David, for his review and contributions.

I want to give special thanks to my friends and financial advisors, Joel Ehrenkranz of Ehrenkranz & Ehrenkranz, Marvin Schwartz of Neuberger Berman and Sandy Gottesman of First Manhattan. They helped me accumulate the funds to use to enjoy giving back to the poor and physically disabled of the world and, in doing so, to find my purpose.

Most of all, I'd like to thank my wife and partner for more than a half a century, Pat, for her support and for putting up with visiting editors, the days away from home as I worked on this book and the boxes of photographs on the kitchen table.

KEB
October 2004

TABLE OF CONTENTS

Appendixes

My Belief
–KEB

It is not the critic who counts. Not the man who points out how the strong man stumbles or where the doer of deeds could have done better. The credit belongs to the man who is actually in the arena, whose face is marred by dust and sweat and blood, who strives valiantly, who errs and comes up short again and again, because there is no effort without error or shortcoming, but who knows the great enthusiasms, the great devotions, who spends himself for a worthy cause; who, at the best, knows, in the end, the triumph of high achievement, and who, at the worst, if he fails, at least he fails while daring greatly, so that his place shall never be with those cold and timid souls who knew neither victory nor defeat.

Theodore Roosevelt

PREFACE

When I was born, people were smiling and I was crying. When I die, I hope that people will cry and I will smile.

Anonymous

I am a simple man who has lived a simple life and, in the process, learned a simple lesson.

I was born poor. But I will die rich—with more money, in fact, than I ever imagined existed when I was boy. By the world's standard, I climbed aboard the American dream and rode it to the top.

Yet as I look back on all my business success, I realize that doing well in business is easy compared with achieving true success: finding a purpose in life beyond just making money. Purpose is something you achieve by giving your heart, time, love and money to provide a better life for mankind—without looking for anything in return.

Our world is filled with men and women who have no true purpose, no calling higher than trying to fill their bank accounts. Some chase money all of their lives, most of the time in vain. Others earn more than they will ever be able to spend, running corporations that will outlive them. Both types of people work away at what they believe is the pursuit of happiness. But they are wrong.

I know how they feel and how they live. My quest for riches blinded me from seeing all that I might be missing. With each moment I filled pursuing an objective I could touch—making money—I had no time to notice that I was missing something that can only be felt.

To be frank, I didn't do well in the world of feelings. But I knew people who did—people who had somehow climbed above the conflict, fear and pressure of pursuing material success and who had discovered what President Abraham Lincoln called the "better angels" of their nature. So I knew it was possible for me to change.

I came to call these fortunate few the "People of Purpose." They are sustained by a mission for a cause greater than themselves, for a direction that gives meaning to their lives. They face each day with conviction and energy, less concerned about the pursuit of wealth and status than they are about living for a larger meaning in their lives.

I have also learned that anyone can become one of the People of Purpose. Membership in this wonderful club is open to all. It is not a birthright; it is not attained by a sudden turn of good fortune or universal popularity; it has nothing to do with money and everything to do with finding and sustaining joy. Not happiness. Joy.

The simple fact is that my own discovery of purpose came long after *Forbes* Magazine listed me as one of the 400 wealthiest men in America. It came after my family was raised—my children grown with children of their own—after I had built cities and owned a professional football team, after I had lived life large in every sense of that modern and misused phrase. It came after I had suffered the irony of believing that those material successes would bring me the fulfillment I so desperately desired.

One of my first glimpses of it came in 2000, when I lifted a small

Vietnamese girl from the ground and placed her in a wheelchair. In that instant, she found hope. In that instant, I saw what happens when one person imprisoned by immobility is finally able to move. I saw this little girl envision a freedom she had never known. Her face opened into a smile, her eyes as bright as the noontime sky. And I knew that for all she had changed in that moment, I had changed even more.

For the first time I could remember, I felt joy. And I wanted to do everything in my power to keep that feeling alive.

Giving her a wheelchair did not cost me my fortune. It did not consume all of my time. What I did was something anyone can do. It was a simple process of opening my heart and allowing it to touch someone else through an act of kindness.

The journey to purpose is not difficult. I believe it begins with something I once heard about people: that we usually travel the path of more, better and different.

We start out wanting more. As children, teens and young adults beginning careers, we are consumed by getting as much as we can as quickly as we can. For me, a child of poverty, it was getting the basic necessities—things as simple as hot water and an indoor bathroom. (One of the reasons I pursued high school football was because school was the first place I could get a hot shower!) Once the basic necessities are covered, we work toward buying our first car, our first house and the rest.

Once we have more, we want better. As mature adults, we have the nice car, perhaps the home and furnishings, a good wardrobe and other amenities. But we are not content, so we seek houses in better neighborhoods, more expensive cars and jewelry, vacations to more exotic destinations.

As time passes and our incomes rise—perhaps the children are raised and out of the house—many of us are still unsatisfied, so we finally turn our attention to acquiring different things: not just the house in the nice neighborhood, but the biggest house in the neighborhood; not just an expensive car, but the most expensive, flashiest car; not just a nice vacation, but a weekend condo at a ski resort.

If we are fortunate enough to accumulate more money than we can spend, we shoot for Lifestyles of the Rich and Famous. We don't want just an expensive house, we want a 10,000-square-foot penthouse on Park Avenue in Manhattan; we don't want just an expensive car, we want the Aston-Martin that James Bond drives in his movies; we don't want just nice vacation, we want a private tour of the Hermitage in St. Petersburg. For me, different was assembling the world's largest classic car collection and buying a National Football League team, a personal yacht and my own private jet, a DC-9.

But no matter how much more, better, different things I accumulated and experienced, I had an empty feeling in my heart. No one had ever discussed or defined purpose to me, but I knew instinctively something was missing. I was selfish and thought "things" would give me pleasure. If I had only known and experienced purpose sooner....

People of Purpose have climbed above more, better and different. They have grown to realize that beyond these three phases of life, there is a fourth—and it is by far the most important: purpose.

I deeply regret wasting so many years before finding purpose—not because I lacked the desire to find what I was looking for, but because I started out thinking it would come through financial achievement. The truth is, I had leaned my ladder against the wrong wall, realizing the mistake only when I was at the top, helplessly aware that, after a career filled with outward success, I did not even know where to look to find real happiness.

My story is one of an average man who achieved extraordinary material success doing a few simple things and then, through a random turn of events, discovered the true fountain of joy.

This is the story of my journey, my discovery. I write it around

the four phases of life described above with the hope that it will help
you, and that you will be able to avoid some of the mistakes I have
made. And I hope that by putting you on the road to purpose and
helping you find your purpose, I can help you to experience joy of
your own to cherish and treasure.

Join me in that most wonderful of places—the place of purpose.

Part I **More**

Chapter 1:
MY FIRST SET OF WHEELS

Be glad of life because it gives you the chance.

Henry Van Dyke

My life began in an elevator of a hospital in Freeport, Illinois, on June 13, 1928. My impatient arrival foreshadowed a recurring theme in my life—never waiting for things to happen, but making things happen.

It was the late 1920s and America was headed into the Great Depression. I was born in Freeport, but I grew up just across the state line in Monroe, Wisconsin. It was a small town made up mostly of Swiss and German Americans. They were from hardworking families with dairy farms that produced some of the best cheese in the world.

My parents' reach for the American Dream did not work out as well as mine did. But their struggle laid the foundation for my later success. They had lost their farm some years before I was born. To provide for our family, my father, Elmer, moved to Monroe to take a job in his brother-in-law's lumberyard. He worked for 25 cents an hour. To make extra money, my mother, Mae, cleaned houses for other families, took in laundry and hung wallpaper with her cousin.

We were poor, but we always had food on the table. Pretty much the same thing every night—fried potatoes and cucumbers. They came from our big garden in the backyard. Sometimes we had meat. We rented a house for $12 a month. The neighborhood was built between the brewery, the cheese factory, a coal yard and the noisy railroad tracks. The house had no hot water or central heat. When my father's dad died, he inherited $1,200. He used that money to buy the house.

My father worked long hours, walking to and from the lumberyard twice a day. It was painful for him—he had a clubfoot that never healed after a botched operation. Even when the temperature dropped to 20 degrees below zero, he would walk in the snow and ice. He came home for lunch because it was the only place he could afford a hot meal.

In the winter, I slept in the cold. A pot-bellied stove in the kitchen was two rooms away, behind two sets of doors. I had only blankets to keep me warm when the temperature outside dropped below zero. If I wanted a hot bath, I had to heat up the water myself on the stove. For much of my childhood, the only clothes I wore were a pair of overalls. Our car was old and did not run most of the time.

Our home was filled with the stress of making ends meet. There was little time for the idle conversation, family activities and affection that bring parents and children together. I think that was the case because my parents were older when I was born. My father was 39, my mother was 32. My sister was older, too—13 years my senior. I was the family tagalong, arriving at a time when my parents were just trying to survive.

They didn't have big dreams. I guess their dreams died when they lost their farm. So I wasn't supposed to dream, either. But I did.

I dreamed of getting out of Monroe someday. I knew there was another world outside my town. I knew that from the newsreels at the movie theater and from Buck Rogers. But my parents said dreams would lead only to disappointment. They told me, "You're poor, Kenneth. You can't do those things you talk about, so forget it." I remember my mother telling me, "You'd better develop a personality. You are not going to make it on your looks." I must have looked hurt, because she turned away quickly, back to her stove.

I can remember every detail about that moment more than 60 years ago. I suppose she was giving me the best advice she could at the time, given our situation and our potential in Monroe. But I also know that my parents weren't equipped to teach me about achieving dreams.

Despite our struggle, I never felt deprived. Almost everybody was in the same boat in the Depression. In fact, I feel I had a happy childhood. I remember the pleasures of small-town life: picnics with relatives; riding with my cousins on the flatbed of my uncle's truck to a lake; spending the day fishing; schoolboy crushes; and going hunting along the railroad track for rabbit, pheasant and squirrel, which provided food for the family. I enjoyed tracking animals and figuring out how to outsmart them; the same with fishing in streams, creeks or lakes nearby.

The only thing that my parents ever forced me to do was study music, take lessons. They chose accordion, of all things. But I thought it was foolish. I kept thinking, "The music lesson money is taking away from our food money." Fortunately, any musical ambitions I might have had ended when I entered the Monroe Music Competition. I was the only accordion player to enter the contest, and the judge awarded me second place. I had to have been pretty bad to win second place in a competition with only one contestant.

The greatest trauma of my childhood was a serious accident. I was 10 years old when a car struck me as I crossed the street. The collision fractured my skull. I was in a coma for a week. I drifted between life and death. When I recovered, I could not remember the accident. The injuries were so serious that I had to learn to walk all over again.

A lot of the conditions of my childhood were beyond my control. But I was not going to let that stop me. I felt special. I felt different from my parents and my neighbors. I wasn't going to let my parents' attitudes prevent me from reaching my goals. We weren't on the same page at any time. They were nice people, but I wasn't proud of them. We rarely talked about anything. I learned to eat fast so I could leave the table and get going.

So I became independent at a very young age. I started making decisions for myself when I was six years old, when I began to work odd jobs. I caught night crawlers and sold them for a nickel a can. As soon as I was old enough to push a lawnmower, I mowed lawns at night and on weekends to earn money. I would approach a neighbor, even strangers, and ask if I could mow the lawn for a quarter—or 50 cents if it was big. I got a job as a caddy at the local golf course. It paid 35 cents a round.

But I really got going as a small businessperson when my parents gave me a bicycle. They cashed in a life insurance policy they had taken out on me when I was born. I didn't care about the life insurance policy—I wanted a bicycle. Really bad. And the policy was the only source of money my parents could tap to enable them to buy me a bike.

It was a big deal. The bike cost $28, a small fortune in the Depression. And it was one of the nicest models—not a cheap one. That was the start of a lifelong pattern—I wanted the best. I didn't want anyone to have a better bicycle. It was a two-tone brown Schwinn with a big basket. It also had a light on the handlebars so I could ride it before dawn. That was important, because it allowed me to make money off my bike. It was the greatest thing that had happened to me to that point.

At 10 years old, I started working for a local cheese maker before school. I would get out of bed around 4 a.m. and bike to the factory. It worked with about 20 farms. Farmers would milk their cows and bring the milk to the factory in large cans. Then I would help the farmers unload the containers. The factory paid me 10 cents an hour.

With that bicycle, I landed my first true job, with the Milwaukee Journal. I got a paper route. I started to sell—one penny for every paper I sold or delivered, two pennies for the Sunday edition.

I began to shape my future. For the first time, I saw how real money was made. And through trial and error, I learned about strategy. Within a short time, I learned to take my load of papers into town and set up sales right outside the drugstore—or as close as I could get without having the owner chase me away. That's where the customers were. At 11 years old, I'd learned my first lesson in business: location, location, location.

That bicycle gave me freedom and mobility for the first time. I could go further, much faster, and I began to appreciate the use of time. Early on, I learned how to be productive. (Little did I know that wheels would also play an important part in my life decades later.) I started giving money to my parents to help them with expenses at home.

I got other jobs. At age 12, I went to work at a local grocery store. At first, I had to stock the shelves. But I begged to do sales. Farmers would bring their eggs to the store and we'd have to count them. Then the farmers would exchange their eggs for groceries. I loved encouraging them to trade their eggs for all the groceries they could take so the store would get as many eggs as possible to resell to other customers. I eventually earned 25 cents an hour in this job, and that was significant: it was the same wage my father was making at the time. Starting at age 14, I made more money loading 50-pound bags of concrete mix from boxcars to trucks in my uncle's lumberyard in the summer. I started out making 25 cents an hour, but eventually I made 50 cents an hour, twice as much as my father. But he never complained to my uncle about his pay; I guess he did not want to risk losing his job.

At age 16, I landed a job at the local Montgomery Ward store. From my work at the grocery store, I knew I loved people and selling. I was good at it, and I could make more money at Montgomery Ward selling on commission. It certainly beat lifting cheese at the cheese factory or loading concrete mix into boxcars. I guess I did a pretty good job in a short time. I wasn't there more than two weeks when the manager put me in charge of two departments, sporting goods and paint.

I always tried to turn a $5 sale into a $100 sale. A customer would come into the store to buy paint for one room and I would say to him, "I think you could make your house worth more if you'd paint the outside. And our paint is a reasonable cost. You can finance it and we'll deliver it to you. You could make your house worth a lot of money." I got a lot of people to paint their barns, too. Or someone would want to buy a cheap fishing reel and I would tell him, "You can't catch a fish with this reel. You need a good reel."

Selling was partly a natural gift. But I also learned quickly never to spend time on people we called "tire-kickers." You could identify them by listening and asking questions. If you got one, you immediately turned him over to someone else. When I got a bona fide customer, I'd learn how much they were willing to spend, also by listening and asking questions. A good salesman talks to a customer only after he listens. I learned to zero in on the customer's needs and then provide the product. I have watched too many salespeople "oversell," meaning that once they got someone ready to purchase, they kept on selling and eventually talked the customer out of buying. Once you write up the order, don't try adding more. You can talk customers right out of their purchases.

Sometimes the store wouldn't stock an item a customer wanted. I knew that was an opportunity for me. I set up my own sporting-goods business on the side. I ran it out of my house. Guns, motors, fishing boats—I knew there was a demand, and I found the supply. On weekends, I'd drive to nearby cities and towns and buy the items at retail. Then I'd come home and resell them to my local customers at a markup. I saw it as not only a good business, but as doing people a favor. I was making more from home than I was at Montgomery Ward.

While I was at it with sporting goods, I started selling cars. I bought my first car, a 1928 Pontiac, for $80 when I was 15. Someone ran into it. I got $100 from the insurance claim and bought used parts to fix it. (I traded my bike for the labor.) I still had the car and traded it for another. I was in business. I'd purchase two wrecked vehicles that were damaged in different areas and have a small body shop rebuild them into one car. Dealing in cars was the first time I could see making money without physical labor.

As soon as I got any money at all, I started another lifelong pattern: buying things. I bought my first car. I bought my parents their first radio. I would look at the catalog in our outhouse, at the guns and fishing poles. I couldn't wait to have a big car, the best fishing pole, the best whatever. I wanted better than I had. As a child growing up in the Depression, my dreams were focused on things that I could acquire or achieve.

I was hungry. When you have less, you are hungrier—for achievement, for things, for success. And that hunger stayed with me all of my life, motivating me to work harder and achieve more. With my bike, my car, my jobs and my ambition, I learned that nothing is impossible.

Even then, I knew I was looking for something. I just didn't know what it was.

Today, I think that I was fortunate to have the parents I had. They gave me what I needed most—independence. Trying to survive in the Depression prevented them from spending time with me. But that gave me the freedom to explore and grow on my own. I learned how to make decisions for myself. I learned a lot quickly. I came to appreciate that there is no meaningless activity, just as there is no meaningless acquaintance. There are no empty actions. I learned that each one led somewhere. And I enjoyed that. I can recall that even before my teenage years, I became aware that activity and relationships led somewhere. I appreciated that idea long before I understood what it was, or what it could do for a person with ambition. That early experience helped me later in business, where leadership and decision-making skills are so critical.

My friends experienced that, too. The difference was that as we grew up, many of them seemed to become satisfied with what they were doing and turned it into a career. Once in a while, I wished I could be satisfied like them. They seemed content. They were good people, hardworking and enjoyable to be with. Many remain close to me today. They were able to settle into comfortable existences. They led lives that were every bit as fulfilling for them as the life I imagined and wanted.

Why couldn't I be content? Even now, a half-century after I first had those feelings, I wonder what it was that has never let me to stop and rest, even for a short time. My father never spoke of unfulfilled dreams. My mother did her best to limit my hopes. My closest relatives were happy in their blue-collar jobs. I didn't learn about dissatisfaction from any of them.

So where did my powerful drive come from? Perhaps from that terrible accident that almost took my life. Perhaps our poverty. Perhaps the lack of love and affection from my parents. I don't know. Whatever the reason, I didn't understand the root of it. In fact, I wouldn't know for another 60 years. All I realized was that I was missing something. At a young age, I began searching for activities and things to fill the void in my heart. I needed to find a sense of fulfillment.

I think it's obvious that my first experience in filling that void came through work. Not only did I feel useful, I felt necessary. I was helping my parents. Work gave me a sense of accomplishment and moving ahead. It gave me a feeling of self-importance. It was as if the harder I worked, the more important I became, to myself and to those who depended me. I also began to learn that the harder I worked, the more fortunate I was.

My work in those early years was menial. Years later, my sons could not understand how I could have been gratified with mowing lawns or carrying golf clubs. I can't blame them. Those jobs were boring and often thankless. But at that point in my life, I performed them with pride and dedication. I knew how I felt when I was working. Time seemed to matter. Actions had consequences. Conditions were changed. At a basic level, lives were improved. There was power in work.

It didn't matter to me what a man did, only that he was a hard worker and was honorable. My father was both. Years later, I came to realize that the difference between us had nothing to do with how hard we worked, or how intelligent we were, or even our abilities. The difference was that I was never satisfied—at least not for long. In time, after every new experience or job, I would become bored. I'd need to explore better opportunities.

I had the freedom to do this because my family did not depend on me as the sole breadwinner. I was able to take risks that my father could not. Already he had lost our farm, and I am sure that event shook his confidence, though we never spoke about it. As he aged, security became more important to him than reward. My father never learned one of my own most important lessons—real reward comes only with risk.

I found freedom in work. But I did not enjoy every minute of every job. There were hours of drudgery, sometimes followed by hours of physical pain. The summer I worked loading the 50-pound bags of concrete mix for my uncle, the temperature inside those boxcars would often climb to more than 100 degrees. We would work long days, resting only once in a while. At night, I'd walk home. My body ached in places that had never ached before. Each morning I'd wake up stiff and sore, counting the days until Sunday, when I could have one day to myself. It was a miserable summer, but the experience proved important to my future. Yet again, the hard work would pay off.

I was a teenager. I was 5 feet, 10 inches and 195 pounds, with short legs and a low center of gravity. The physical labor hardened me, increasing my coordination and power. The bad working conditions disciplined me to heat and exhaustion. I learned not to complain. I just did my job.

I don't know how I made it through that summer. But when fall arrived, I had the opportunity to join the football team. And I was ready. For all of the boredom and pain, that summer job was one of the most important experiences of my young life. I didn't realize it at the time, but my hard labor was preparing me for a success that, more than anything up to that point in my life, would define who I was and what I would become.

Chapter 2:
THE PLAYING FIELD

Build up your weaknesses
until they become your strong points.

Knute Rockne

I learned a lot about life from football. As a teenager, I loved the game. I couldn't wait from one season to the next. Football gave me satisfaction. It let me use my inborn ability. It built my competitiveness. And for the first time, my peers and older people alike recognized me. I liked that then, and I still do.

But football gave me much more.

Football was big in Monroe, one of the few diversions people in a small town could enjoy. At 195 pounds, I was the biggest player on my team, the Monroe High "Cheesemakers." I was strong and a good sprinter. "Built for football," my yearbook said. On offense, I was a running back, and on defense, I was a linebacker. And I loved to hit. I learned that intimidation was a great advantage on the field. I found out that if you hit your opponents harder than they hit you,

you never got hurt.

I wasn't the best athlete, but I gave 120 percent every time I played. I always played 60 minutes of each contest. I never came out. One time, I was stuck in bed with a bad flu. But our game that week was against the best team in the conference. I climbed out of bed and went to the field. My teammates were afraid I wasn't going to make it, but my showing up gave them more confidence. I didn't play my best that day, but it was enough to help our team win.

I developed my competitiveness in sports early on—hunting, fishing, swimming. When I was 10, I played sports with a girl from a wealthy family in town. She was a year older than I was, a tomboy and a terrific athlete. She was tougher than anyone I ever played. I had to work hard to keep up with her. If she beat me at tennis, I'd keep coming back. I'd watch her playing tennis with her friends, try-ing to zero in on her weaknesses. She taught me to try harder and to uncover opponents' weak spots. Eventually, I found hers and learned to beat her.

I had a high tolerance for pain. The hot boxcars of my summer job had taught me not to think about it. I could control it. I thought positively. I took all of that to the football field and discovered that long practices and hard work didn't wear me down like it did my teammates. I enjoyed practices. I often felt more energy afterward than before they began. I hated games to end. I guess this showed in my attitude, because I was captain of the team before long. I was often in the headlines of the local sports page. Behring Named Among Wisconsin Grid Leaders, one headline read.

For some reason, in my freshman season, I purchased the largest pair of shoes I could find. They were five sizes too big. I stuffed the toes with cotton to try to make them fit. I don't know what I was thinking. Halfway through the season, my coach took me out of play in the middle of a game. He ordered me to remove my ridiculous "clown shoes" and put on a smaller pair that fit. He took the smaller shoes from one of my teammates and just gave them to me. My performance improved immediately.

Maybe I wanted those larger shoes because they made me feel bigger and more important. I will leave that to the psychologists to decide. But I'm sure those oversized shoes tell more about my personality back then than I really want to know.

Our playbook was not sophisticated. I would say it was four yards and a cloud of dust, except that football seasons in Wisconsin were mostly mud. I soon learned that my short legs gave me the competitive advantage. I had better leverage to go head to head in the mud. I was given the ball two out of four downs and sent crashing through the line—right and left—over the guards and tackles, or around the end. I used to fight for every inch. One game, the rain and mud were so thick that the other team wanted to cancel. My coaches insisted we continue; they understood our advantage in the mud. I ran for a record that night, even though the other team targeted me. The defense tackled me on every down, whether I had the ball or not.

In those days, natural ability was about all anybody had. We didn't have the sophisticated training tools athletes use today. There were no weight rooms, no trainers, no dietary supplements or cross-training strategies. But there were hot showers. Football provided me, for the first time in my life, with a hot shower. I knew about hot water and indoor plumbing, naturally. But we didn't have that in our home. We had the old water pump in the front yard. It provided two things: cold water for the family and a place to tie up Butch, my pointer. He never learned to point to the day he died.

One player, Eugene Davis, taught me that natural ability isn't required for success. At 135 pounds, Eugene didn't fit the mold of a classic football player. Physically, you'd think he was better suited for the chess team—a fair-haired kid with intense concentration. But Eugene's build and look were only part of the story.

His heart was bigger than Lake Michigan. As a blocking back, he would throw himself against bigger opponents on the line. He didn't seem to care about hurting himself. He'd open up holes for me to run through, then return to the huddle to get his instructions and do it all over again. I can't remember Eugene carrying the ball my entire senior year, and I can't remember him once complaining. With his small size in the offensive backfield, and playing cornerback on defense, he reminded me many times of a killer bee: out of nowhere, he would come up and sting players more than twice his size. Sometimes he'd lay them out flat.

Often the most tenacious and successful people will be those you least expect, those who play from the heart. Eugene was the first person I met who helped me understand this. Since then, I've come to recognize the quality of an exceptional heart almost instantly. There is something in the individual's face, a clear-eyed honest enthusiasm that becomes infectious to the rest of the team.

Football games were rarely physically painful for me. I had those hot boxcars to thank for that. But they were emotionally painful, at first. It seemed that about everybody came out to support the team—except my parents.

It upset me that my parents didn't attend my games. The school gave players free tickets for parents. I would leave them on the kitchen table at home and mention them to my mother and father. Early on, I would search the stands, hoping they would be there. But they never came. I was disappointed and hurt.

But in hindsight, I can't blame them. My dad was tired when he came home. He couldn't leave work early for games because couldn't afford to lose his 25-cents-an-hour job. For one thing, we were always in debt to the grocery store. A few years later, I found out that my parents never got ahead of their food debts and that they still owed money to the grocer. (I paid off that bill myself.)

So after a while, I stopped looking for them in the stands. I reminded myself that they really couldn't afford free time. But from that experience, I started to think about money and the freedom it could buy. Long before I was successful, I knew from the experience of missing my parents at games that time and money were connected: Not only is time money, but money provides time.

Football also taught me about leadership. I was bigger than my teammates, so that helped me take charge. And I wanted to take charge. I wasn't the quarterback, but I basically called the shots. Our quarterback, a friend of mine, was a good athlete and a good guy. But I was afraid he wasn't going to call on me often enough, and I wanted the ball every down. In the huddle, if he made a call I didn't like, I would override him. The other players would just go along with it. I wanted to be in every play. I loved running.

I must have learned something on the field. On Valentine's Day 1946, our schoolmates gathered in the gym to honor our team for winning the conference championship my senior year. Our coach, Howard Sharp, and principal, T.R. Holyoke, handed out miniature golden football trophies and varsity letters. It was nice to be recognized.

I also exercised leadership off the field. I am not especially proud of one experience. But I learned something from that, too.

We had three months until graduation. We felt things slowing down, including our phys-ed classes. Because we were so close to the coaches through sports, gym class was pretty informal. It was the end of the year. We were bored. Our coaches looked the other way. So my friends and I often skipped gym to cross the street to a local bar.

One spring day, however, we got a little too comfortable at the bar. We all had maybe one too many beers. Time got away from us. Before we knew it, gym was over and we were late to our next period. By the time we showed up at class, we were doing our best to keep the smell of alcohol off our breath. But our teacher wouldn't let us into the room. Whether someone had told her where we had been or whether she simply knew from our behavior, I can't remember. But I do recall that she demanded we leave. She suspended us for our behavior.

I should have accepted my punishment and returned to school the following day, sorry for my behavior. I deserved to be suspended. But I was arrogant and full of myself. I took the leadership skills I had developed in the three previous years and came up with a plan to get back at the school. With a friend, Harold Davidson, I organized a strike—a student walkout. But not to protest my suspension—I knew my classmates wouldn't go for that.

I found a better cause. Earlier, the school had announced that Coach Sharp was going to be let go to make room for Coach Don Huddleston, who was returning from the war. It was a commitment the school had made to Coach Huddleston, though Coach Sharp had taken us to the conference championship. And it was a commitment the school was going to keep.

I knew there was enough support among my classmates to organize a strike on behalf of Coach Sharp. And that's what I did. Word spread instantly. The next day, the town square filled with hundreds of students marching, chanting and holding signs. They demanded that the school keep Coach Sharp.

It was dishonest; it was wrong. But it succeeded in keeping the students out of class for days, at least until our school superintendent, E. O. Evans, called me to his office. He asked me to call off the strike and get students back to school.

While I had initiated the strike under false pretenses, I did learn a valuable lesson from Superintendent Evans. The walkout had embarrassed him and challenged his leadership. But he didn't get angry or confront me. Instead, he approached me on two more effective levels: he appealed to our personal relationship and he appealed to my reason.

His son was a friend of mine. I'd spent many hours at the Evans home, and the superintendent had always been kind to me. He began our conversation by reminding me of that relationship. He put my actions and their consequences within that framework. He got me to agree that we did have a good relationship and that we could be considered friends. Then he got to the heart of the issue: a commitment had been made to Coach Huddleston.

The coach had served our country in the war and brought honor to Monroe. Superintendent Evans had made him a promise. I couldn't argue. I was about to back off when he made his final point. I was surprised. It forced me to surrender completely.

Evans said he knew what had happened the day I called the strike. He'd spoken with the teacher. He knew my motives were wrong. But then he made me an offer I couldn't refuse. He said he'd let me back into class without further punishment for my trip to the bar. I agreed. The strike was over. Students returned to school. But my regret through the years about the incident was magnified by that fact that in the end, Don Huddleston never came back to Monroe. I don't know why. But I have often wondered whether it was because of the strike and my bad behavior. If it was, I want to sincerely say now, "I'm sorry, Coach."

Since then, I've observed that a charismatic personality who's willing to take risks only for personal gain does not make a good leader. Principle-centered leadership is based on selfless courage, practical wisdom and moral objectives. It's based on honesty and focused on achieving what is best for others, whether they understand it or not. Consequently, great leaders are not always popular, but they are consistent. Opinion polls, conventional wisdom and difficult endeavors don't affect them. Their vision exceeds the horizon, and they have the ability to put momentary action and current affairs in a larger, more meaningful context.

Though these lessons have been often repeated, they made their first and most indelible impression on the Monroe High School football field. I was about to begin applying them in the "real" world.

Chapter 3:
THE CHICKEN COOP

*The man who will use his skill
and constructive imagination to see how much
he can give for a dollar, instead of how little he can
give for a dollar, is bound to succeed.*

Henry Ford

My plan out of high school was to play football at the University of Wisconsin. I had been encouraged by a coach to compete at the college level. My friend Harold Davidson and I invested $35 in a tiny trailer that we pulled behind a car to Madison. We parked in the back of a service station near campus, paying the owner $3 a month to supply us with water, electricity and a bathroom.

Madison was beautiful in the fall. The campus was busy. I enjoyed being part of a big college football program. But my college career ended quickly. In preseason training, I blew out my knee. Without the chance of an athletic scholarship, I knew staying at school would be almost impossible. The war had ended and upper-classmen were returning from service; financial aid was hard to come by. I just didn't have the resources to stay. I dropped out after one semester. My decision to move on became easier in winter, when our trailer became an icebox. The heater could take only enough fuel to stay on for three hours at most. It was almost impossible to sleep at night.

Quitting college was a big turning point in my life. It was one of the few times I felt indecision. I almost gave it one more try: one of my freshman coaches was a former colonel in the Marine Corps and had graduated from the Naval Academy in Annapolis. He suggested I transfer there, rather than give up on college altogether. I had passed the university athletic program's toughest physical exam, so I felt I could handle Annapolis. And it seemed like a good idea to go. So I hit the road. I drove 300 miles before I had a change of heart. I turned around and drove back home to Monroe. On a stretch of road somewhere, I realized I couldn't live under the tight restrictions of college, let alone a military school. I knew then I wanted to get to work and make money. I knew I wanted to go into business for myself and would never work for a corporation, so I really didn't need a college degree anyway. And I was impatient—I didn't want to wait three and a half years to start my career.

Before I left school, I managed to complete a few courses. One was "City Planning." The professor asked me if I had transferred from another college, as he hadn't seen me on campus before. I replied that I was a freshman. He was shocked—he told me the class was only for seniors. But he let me stay. For one assignment, I planned a complete city. Later on in life, I would build a city from scratch in Florida. I guess I got something out of college after all.

I have no regrets about my limited college experience except for one thing: I miss the network of friends and classmates that stays in touch after graduation. And I did finally get a degree—an honorary doctorate from Brigham Young University in 2002, in recognition of my philanthropy and business success.

After high school, one of my best friends, Dick Bienema, took off to join the Coast Guard. Like me, he needed to make his own way in life. He, too, had grown up on the wrong side of the tracks. After his mother died, his father married a woman who refused to raise Dick because he served as a reminder of the previous wife. Dick's father had a good job and could have taken care of him. But the new wife would not allow it, and he was shipped to his grandparents in Monroe. They lived on public assistance.

Dick became an immediate friend through school. We met when we got into an argument over who would play a position on the softball team. His great personality and his sense of adventure impressed me. He had been cut off from his father. He watched stepbrothers and stepsisters receive the love and opportunities that he would never know. But he refused to let that defeat him. He simply kept moving forward in his life. After the Coast Guard, he got a good job as a mason.

Dick and other friends beginning their careers inspired me. I assessed my professional options. Outside of football, my passion was cars. My years working at Montgomery Ward and my experience trading cars had taught me how to sell, how to read customers, how to focus on their needs and help them make the necessary connections to complete a sale. So I decided to become an automobile salesman.

A friend of mine who had worked with me at Montgomery Ward had left for a job at the local Hudson dealership. She got a hold of me when she heard I was back in town, telling me that the dealer was desperate for a good salesman. But Hudsons were not easy to sell (they were one of the biggest product bombs in the history of American business). So six months later, I went to work for the local Chevrolet dealer. For my dollar, Chevrolet was manufacturing the best cars in 1948 and 1949, including the line of trucks that were in demand in Monroe. The owner paid me a 25 percent commission on gross profit and included me on business decisions. He allowed me to travel, buy new cars from other dealers and bring them back to

Monroe. My lifelong interest in cars gave me a good eye for what customers wanted. Soon, I was making more in commissions than his son and son-in-law, who managed the dealership. They decided to cut my commissions from gross profits to net profits (after overhead), which cut my paycheck by half. I decided to quit. They were left without their top salesman, and their business suffered. There was a saying in Monroe: "You feed the pigs, but you send the hogs to market." They had gotten greedy, and now they were suffering the consequences.

After two years with the Chevy dealership, I moved to a Chrysler dealership. Ernest Studer, a hardworking and honest man with a large family, owned it. He also gave me the latitude to buy inventory. I also managed the used car business. But I soon realized that his first love was farm machinery, and his objective was to get out of car sales. So I knew there was also no future there.

I knew one thing for sure: I was disappointed in working for others. So I had an idea for my own company, Behring Motors. Now, at age 21 and four years out of high school, I felt I could not rely on somebody else for my living. I wanted to do what I wanted to do, as fast as I could. My employers had not been fast movers. I had learned this in a short time: Most people think about things and then do them. I do things and then think about them. Ready, fire, aim. I realized I would not be as successful as I wanted to be working for someone else.

My father had worked for others. I admired him in a way. He was a good employee and a stable provider. When I worked for the Chevy and Chrysler dealerships, I tried to be the kind of employee my father had been, always there, always on time. And I quickly came to appreciate the feeling of security. I could have stayed with them forever and made a good living. The Chevy dealership was paying me almost $10,000 a year, a nice income in Monroe in the 1940s.

It was also plenty to support a wife and family. I had known Pat

Riffle briefly in high school. She had dated my good friend Jerry Schwaiger and had set me up on a double date with her friend. But her friend and I didn't click, and I resented her a bit for putting me with someone I wasn't interested in. Fifty years later, Jerry, Pat and I still get together.

After high school, Pat worked upstairs in the accounting office at Montgomery Ward. I worked the floor in sales and counted every commission in my head even before a sale was completed. On payday, I could estimate to within a dime how much my paycheck would be. I got angry at Pat one payday when the check came up short. Standing above her desk, I all but accused her of cheating me out of my commission. I was impressed when she smiled and calmly answered that she would look into it immediately and, if there was a problem, take care of it directly. There was a problem. She fixed it.

I was too impulsive to be embarrassed, but not too embarrassed to ask her out after my return from college. She had been dating a friend of mine, the son of Monroe's chief of police. But that didn't stop me. Our first date was a dance at Lake Delvin. The woods were cool, and the dance floor was lit up by lightbulbs strung post to post. A big band played popular songs by Tommy Dorsey, Artie Shaw and Glenn Miller. As she had that day in her office, Pat impressed me with her confidence. She seemed at ease with me. She did not appear too impressed, either. I mean, I was the top-selling car salesman in Monroe—perhaps even the county! And I now drove one of the nicer cars—a bright yellow 1948 Buick convertible I had bought a year earlier. She was quiet, but she seemed genuinely interested in me and my observations about life.

We enjoyed the evening together. But she surprised me when I pulled up in front of her house. She immediately jumped out and ran inside—not even a "good night." I wasn't used to that. I pulled away from the curb wondering what I had done. Did I miss something? Hadn't we had a good time? As I drove away, I went over the evening in my mind, the conversations and activity. Had I said something wrong? Not paid enough attention to her? Did one of my friends say something?

She solved the mystery the following morning. She called to apologize for her abrupt departure—she said she'd simply gone too long without a powder room break. I said I understood and asked her out a second time. She accepted, and we continued our romance through the summer. Her stepmother warned her about my type. "I wouldn't fall in love with him," she said. "All he'll do in life is hunt and fish and go bald." She was right on every account. Despite her concerns, Pat and I fell in love. We were married on October 16, 1949. She was 20 and I was 21.

From the beginning, it was clear that Pat was the only girl for me. She was supportive in every way, willing to do whatever I needed, providing me with freedom and flexibility. I would need it as I made plans to build my own used car dealership, from the hubcaps up.

I talked the Chevy dealership into selling me the 27 cheapest used cars on its lot for $900. I paid for them out of my savings. They were anything but luxury cars. But at least I had a starting inventory I could afford.

My first challenge was finding a suitable lot, inexpensive but well located. I found it on a section of highway on the edge of town. I rented it from the owner for $100 a month. It was cheap, but that's because it was located in lowland. I needed to build up the ground to road level before it was suitable for a car lot.

Without much money to fill in the property, I had an idea: homebuilders in Monroe were digging out basements for new construction. They were hauling the excavated dirt away and dumping it. What if I could convince them not only to give me the dirt, but also to pay me for a place to dump it, on my lot? I contacted several builders, and to my surprise, they agreed. And the money they paid me, $25 a truckload, actually gave me enough cash to buy gravel to put over the fill.

Soon I had my lot upgraded and ready for the chicken coop that would serve as my office.

Yes, a chicken coop. I bought it for $25 from a local farm. I knew the son of the farmer, and the price included delivery. When it arrived, the inside was caked with dried chicken manure as hard as concrete. The smell was almost unbearable. I scraped and cleaned the inside walls for days. I stepped outside only long enough to catch my breath, clear my lungs and grab some fresh air. It was a job that I would never have done for anyone else. But the vision of what the coop would become kept me going. I remember it all so vividly that I can still see and smell it today.

Then I went to work with paint. I remember feeling that with each stroke of the 10 coats I put on the walls, I was a step closer to a new opportunity, even a new life. I laid linoleum on the wooden floors. Outside, I used what I had learned while working in the electrical department at Montgomery Ward to install some lighting. I strung bulbs together to hang from four-by-four posts that I had set into the ground around the lot.

I decided to paint the exterior of the coop red and white to catch people's attention from the road. The sign read "Behring Motors." Inside the coop, I had only one lightbulb in the ceiling. But it was my first office. There was no clock to watch, no division of duties, no delegation. I couldn't take off weekends and holidays. It all came down to me, and it was all I could think about.

Suddenly, I was in business. Initially, business was good. I sold my first car, a 1931 Oldsmobile, for $100 just two days after I opened my lot.

But some big challenges came quickly. Within a few months, the rainy season began. And the rain came down. It mixed with the fill I had so cleverly gotten the homebuilders to pay me to dump. I had not put down enough gravel. Before long, the lot was little more than a mud patch. I could not walk without sinking up to my knees in mud. My cars were stuck. The lightpoles tipped; the lights sagged. Would anyone stop to buy a car from me? My competition was not suffering the same way. More than once, I thought of the Chevy dealership, of the warmth of a "real" office and security of a "real" business.

But that muddy fall turned out to be a bump in the road. Fortunately, there were a few customers who were able to look beyond the appearance of my business to find a good car at a good price, and I was able to make ends meet. Eventually, I had the lot back in shape. More fill dirt. More gravel. Cement bases to secure the light poles. My bank began working with me to buy find better used cars, and I discovered a market that other dealers weren't willing to serve—customers with no credit history. So I began to finance car purchases on my own. I would sell a $500 car to a customer for $75 down and $25 a month until it was paid off. Things were looking up. Pat and I had started to build a house so we could move from our apartment.

Then winter came. I knew it was important to winterize my 50 cars in inventory. But I had just rebuilt my lot and had spent most of my capital. To winterize meant that I needed to buy alcohol or antifreeze, put it in the radiators and run it through the engine of each car. However, I was low on cash and hoped to preserve as much as I could for as long as I could. I had put off winterizing my cars.

Bad move.

One morning, I woke up to a bitter cold. An arctic front had rolled into Monroe overnight. The radio said that by evening, the temperature would fall to well below zero. I rushed out to find enough alcohol to winterize my cars. That was no easy task—everyone else in town was buying alcohol for their cars, and there wasn't much in stock at the stores. Each moment I wasted running around to find it was precious, as I had no one to help me get all 40 cars ready by nightfall. The future of Behring Motors and my dreams looked bad.

By the time I was back on the lot, the skies were dark gray. The lot was whipped by a wicked wind, which made being outside almost unbearable. With every car, I had to crawl underneath, my back flat against the frozen gravel, and struggle with cold, dry and often rusted drain cocks. I had no garage. I had no specialized tools. My hands quickly froze beyond feeling. My knuckles become battered and bloodied as my pliers slipped on stubborn bolts. There was little room to move beneath the cars, and when I finally managed to open a drain, ice-cold water poured over my hands and face and soaked my coat and clothes.

I worked as fast as I could. I began with the most expensive cars, just in case I couldn't finish the job before it was too late and before the freeze ruined the remaining cars. By late afternoon, the schools were letting out. I drove to the high school and hired two teenagers to help me. The temperature was below zero. There was not a lot of time left. My fingers were stiff and my back ached. I went home for 10 minutes to change my clothes. But back at the lot, I still could not wear gloves because the bolts and drains that needed loosening were small and required as much nimbleness as my frozen hands could muster. Within an hour, I was soaked again, as water continued to gush out of the drains and flow up my sleeves, over my face and down my neck. But one by one, we worked to drain the radiators and the engines. Then we'd pour in the alcohol and start the cars to circulate it through the engines.

After nightfall, the temperature was 16 degrees below zero. We had managed to save 25 cars but still had 25 to go. Every movement was painful. As it got colder, many cars would not start, so we couldn't get the alcohol running through the engines. It was slow going. We had to tow some cars a few yards to jump-start them with the clutch.

My mind raced as I scrambled to save my business. My dreams could not end here. I had always believed I'd see them through.

There was no such thing as something that couldn't be done. You'd run into problems, but I believed everything was curable. I realized I needed to plan ahead to survive in business. I should have put more effort into borrowing the money to pay for winterizing. When you are on your own, you have to take care of everything yourself. In whatever business you are in, there will be problems, so you might as well fix them as they happen because no one else will fix them for you. It takes initiative, sometimes everything you have, to fix the problem.

I climbed under yet another car and then another, struggling to open the drains. I moved more slowly, painfully, pouring in the alcohol, getting the engine started and then moving down the line. Unable to work any longer in the bitter conditions, my hired help went home. I stayed on. The air was so cold that the water draining onto my face and hands and arms and chest froze, despite my body heat. My hands were a mess, red and raw, barely able to grip my tools. The only thing I could feel through the blood was the sting of the alcohol, spilling on me as I worked. By midnight, I realized that I would never get to all the cars in time. Some cars would be lost. It was going to be an expensive lesson in procrastinating and failing to invest money when it was needed. I worked another five hours, to 6 a.m., until I had winterized all but the least expensive cars on the lot. The engines and radiators on the remaining few were already frozen. I would have to sell them for scrap.

I pulled myself from beneath the last car I knew I could save and looked around. I wondered if I could recover from the loss. I turned toward my chicken coop. And that's what it was at that moment—a chicken coop. Not an office. Not the future of Behring Motors. Not even a good investment. The only light was coming from the cheap bulbs I had strung together and hung myself—cheap bulbs dangling over a gravel lot with a bunch of old cars. How could things get any worse?

It started to snow.

We had a few days to move the ruined cars off the lot and get a little cash for them from the junkyard. I sold another few cars to paying customers, which gave me enough working capital for a month. With a little sleep, I went back to work. I was not going to give up. Behring Motors was more than just a business; it was my stake in a brighter future.

That winter, Monroe was hit with one of the biggest snowfalls I can remember. More than three feet of snow fell in a matter of days, and business came to a near standstill. My cars were locked on the lot, buried in snow. The snowplows had piled five- and six-foot banks on either side of the highway, making it impossible for anyone to get in or out of my lot, including me. There were no customers. Again, I was low on money. I was not sure how to proceed, or if I could.

All I knew is that I could not sit by and do nothing. My lot needed to be cleared. Without selling a car or two, I would be in trouble, and the bad weather was settling in. In fact, the only real business moving in Monroe appeared to be the snowplows. No sooner had that thought crossed my mind than I saw an opportunity: I was not the only businessman suffering from bad weather. Everyone in Monroe was. We all needed the same thing, and there was a premium for those who could provide it.

Without enough cash to pay someone to clear my lot, I bartered with a man in town who owned a surplus Army Jeep with four-wheel drive and a plow. I traded him a truck and car. With the Jeep and plow, I went to work clearing my lot and cleaning up my inventory. Still, there were no customers. So Behring Motors diversified. For the next several weeks, I drove the streets of Monroe from 6 a.m. until 11 p.m., looking for any opportunity to make a few dollars by plowing out driveways and business parking lots. It was not part of my original business plan. In fact, it was an accidental opportunity— the result of creative desperation. I realized then, while still in my twenties, that survival, if not success itself, rests in a person's ability to think beyond the current situation.

Too many people, because of their current condition—whether from family challenges, decline of their business or problems with their health—become unable to explore the possibilities that might be right in front of them. Others are simply too complacent or even lazy to see the snow all around them—snow that is killing their business—and realize that that snow may actually be an opportunity just waiting for them to exploit.

In fact, I've learned that within every setback, there's opportunity. You just have to think outside the box to see it. That was true back in Monroe and it's still true today. In any business you go into, you should think, "How can I make opportunity from that setback?" Because someone else always gains from a setback. In a successful business, you should try to be that person.

The weeks of falling snow had threatened to put me into early bankruptcy. It turned into a gift after I traded an old truck and car for a snowplow. With the new perspective of a plowman, I found myself actually hoping for the next snowfall and then the next, knowing that I could resume selling cars in the spring. But until then, I had guaranteed work. I was not going to be sitting alone in my chicken coop worrying about a run of bad luck putting me out of business.

All the time I spent driving the snowplow, I never lost my vision for Behring Motors. If anything, the experience gave me a new perspective and greater energy. It also gave me the chance to meet hundreds of people I had never met before. They hired me to plow their driveways,. The relationships we built as I returned with each new snowfall eventually found many of them coming to see me in spring to buy something to put back in their driveways. They not only became customers of my snowplow business but soon looked to me when they wanted to buy a car.

I could close a sale pretty fast, because people wanted to get out of the smell of my office. Looking back, I can only imagine what people must have thought as they passed my little lot, seeing me, in my early twenties, standing ankle deep in mud with customers, looking at used cars. But to me, Behring Motors was never a used car lot. It was the first realization of my dreams. It was freedom, a destination and a voyage. I was making my own decisions. Success or failure would be my responsibility. Behring Motors was more than a livelihood. It was a school where I continued to learn principles that would allow me to build my business.

I made some mistakes, largely due to my own greed. One I still regret, from my days as a Hudson salesman, was inflating the price of a junk car I sold to a kid who I took as an easy mark. The car actually belonged to a friend of mine, and, as a favor to him, I made the sale through the dealership, with the owner's permission. The sale was easy—too easy. The finance company was happy to make the loan, because the dealership guaranteed it. But when the kid didn't make his monthly payments—he probably never intended to—the finance company repossessed the car. It was in terrible shape, half wrecked. I could have stuck the dealer with the mess, but I didn't, paying the finance company myself. (The dealer was a nice guy who had been trying to help me and had done my friend a favor.) As they said in Monroe, "You feed the pigs, but you send the hogs to market." My greed butchered my personal finances.

I soon realized that successful transactions are win-win and that strong financial foundations are built slowly, and built to last. I learned to be much more careful in sales. I still had to sell junk cars from time to time, but I sold them at junk prices, not inflated ones. I learned you can't sell someone something for more than they can afford. The truth is no one is ever successful if he takes advantage of people. A deal has to be fair for all parties. You can't take advantage of someone just because they don't know better. That philosophy turned out to be good for business. Because I treated people fairly, the word got out in the community that I was a good person to deal with.

My client base was growing. With warmer weather, I was able to move my inventory and invest in better cars. My work through the winter, and my ability to save the business, improved my reputation and my credibility with the bank. I was now a trusted client. Soon, the bank let me borrow money against the finer used cars I purchased for inventory. At the time, consumer interest rates were high, at double digits. But my banker, Roland Blaha, was willing to lend me money at 6 percent. He taught me the awesome potential of financing.

My favorable bank relationship allowed me to enter the finance business. I'd sell my cars and finance them at a market interest rate and repay the bank at its lower "best customer" rate. Soon, I found that I could make more money through financing than by selling. It was also beneficial for my customers, many of whom couldn't afford to buy a car outright or were struggling with bad credit.

Again, Roland's faith in me paid dividends, as he and the bank backed all of my loans. It was the same faith he had demonstrated years earlier when, for no apparent reason, he had allowed me at 17 to sign the financing for my own car. Most people could not take out a car loan until they were 21. But for some reason Roland believed in me. He was willing to finance anything I proposed, and I often wonder where I would be today had he not been so willing to take the risks he did. In fact, there were times when he brought the ideas to me. He convinced me some years later to build the first apartments in Monroe, a small number of units that he taught me how to secure with federal guarantees.

With Roland's support, I gradually learned that success comes through seeing how much you can give the consumer for his money, not from worrying about how much of his money you can get. Behring Motors grew faster than anyone could have predicted. People knew they would pay a fair price and that I would look out for them and provide affordable financing. That financing, in turn, provided something new and wonderful for me: the stability of reoccurring income. Every month, hundreds of people would sit down and write checks to Behring Motors. That steady income allowed me to take my next step.

I wanted to open a second location. I invited my father-in-law, H.W. "Budd" Riffle, to join the expanding business. Budd was a colorful and warm personality who loved music and dancing. He was a devoted father and had actually been a golfing friend of mine before I began dating his daughter. In Monroe, he had built a career as an advertising manager at the local newspaper. But like me, he wanted to be his own boss and build his own future.

With Behring Motors established, we opened Ken-Budd Used Car Sales on the other side of town. Budd was a natural with customers, as well as a good partner. Our solid customer relationships led to further business development, and before long we were moving into new cars, including foreign imports. We believed in aggressive sales tactics, advertising and participating in community organizations.

Meanwhile, the money I was earning by moving better inventory and providing financing allowed me to relocate Behring Motors from my disadvantaged outdoor location to a lot in town with a garage. It was the old Studebaker dealership, which had gone out of business. I rented it month to month. I hired my first salesmen, Dick Bienema, my friend from high school who was back from the Coast Guard. Dick and I worked hard, seven days a week, from 8 in the morning until 11 at night. Our financing operation grew to include auto insurance.

Sales were so strong that within a few years, Ford Motors contacted me about opening the first Lincoln-Mercury dealership in Monroe. We tried to lease the Studebaker building for it, but the owner would not rent it to us long term. Again, I had to come up with a creative solution to a problem. Through my bank, I found a farmer who would lend me enough money to buy the material for the garage. Luckily, I found a lot on the edge of town and was able to talk Dick Bienema and my other employees into doing the labor to build the garage while I made enough money selling cars to maintain their salaries. We went to auction and bid on equipment to use for construction. Although it was an ambitious plan, somehow we completed the garage and opened for business in less than a year.

In 1953, Behring Motor Company became Behring Lincoln-Mercury, and our decision paid off. Within two years, we were exceeding our quota of new car sales by more than 800 percent. One month, we outsold the combined total sales of the six Chevrolet and four Ford dealerships in the county. We were using every form of promotion we could think of. We announced a contest: whoever stood in a line the longest would win a $300 used car. It was summer; there were a lot of flies. The people standing in line got to see all of our cars, and the people driving by on the highway saw all the people standing in line. It was a great public relations stunt that made the local newspaper. Someone stood there for five days to win that car.

We were known as the "crazy people." We were horse traders—literally. We took riding horses, motorcycles, milk machines—even watches—in trade. Our pitch was that if customers could come up with enough value in a trade in to make a down payment, we would finance the rest of the purchase. Of course, we took cash for down payments, too.

Other dealers didn't like our tactics very much because in their eyes, we weren't quite legitimate. We felt we were just being innovative. Dealerships were largely family businesses back then; sons took over from their fathers and did exactly what was done before. We came in and blew them out of the water. We held high-profile promotions. We started the discounting and everyone had to follow. We were open to 11 p.m. each day and open Sundays. Every other dealer closed at 6 p.m. and on Sundays. For us, it was a seven-day-a-week job. The only day we closed was Christmas. It proved once again to me that the harder you work, the more fortunate you are.

About then, I had another close call with my life. The first had been that childhood car accident. This time, I almost died because of my love of sports and speed. My friends and I liked to build small speedboats and race them on local lakes. One day in 1954, I was working on a boat in our service garage. I didn't know it, but gasoline fumes were building up under the hood. When I climbed into the seat and tested the starter, BOOM, the boat exploded. I don't remember anything about it. But my friends said the explosion threw me 100 yards in a ball of flame. The blast also blew out two plate glass windows in the showroom. I was burned over more than 80 percent of my body. It was very painful. Fortunately, there was a doctor nearby. He made me immediately drink salt water, which helped protect my burned skin. I was in the hospital only two or three days. When I walked back into work, our bookkeeper almost passed out. I did not look good.

I had always felt that guardian angels watched over me. This was the second time I had cheated death. Higher powers wanted to keep me around for some purpose.

Part II **Better**

Chapter 4:
THE SUNSHINE STATE

Behold the turtle. He makes progress
only when he sticks his neck out.

James Bryant Conant

Three years after starting Behring Lincoln-Mercury, I was a 27-year-old making $50,000 a year and I had a million dollars in assets. Monroe was getting smaller. I looked around and became aware that some people still had more than I did. I wasn't satisfied. I was tired of the car business after a decade of selling them.

My father-in-law, Budd, had retired from our used car business three years earlier. He made retired life look very attractive. Both he and I had become golf nuts, and I was intrigued by the prospects of a quiet life dedicated to perfecting my game. Perhaps this was the chance. In 1956, I decided to sell my dealership to Dick Bienema and Lloyd Siedschlag, another friend I had convinced to join the business. I kept only the finance operation and the building. I also still owned rental apartments. With income from investments and the sale of the dealership, I had more than enough money to retire in

Florida, and at that moment, that's what I thought I might do. In the late 1940s, we had vacationed there. Coming from Wisconsin, where winter temperatures hit 30 degrees below, the sunshine and beaches of Florida seemed like paradise.

I also knew there was opportunity in the Sunshine State. Ford had approached me about opening another Lincoln-Mercury dealership in Miami, and a fellow auto dealer had recommended Fort Lauderdale, an up-and-coming city north of Miami. To check things out, I sent one of my most enterprising employees, Bob Trachsel, down to explore the state. I trusted Bob. He was industrious and loyal. Like most of those who joined my team, he had come from poverty; he began to work at a filling station as soon as he was old enough. Tall and skinny, Bob was five years younger than I was. I had hired him right out of high school. More than anything, he was dependable, and I took his recommendation. After some looking around, Bob agreed there might be good opportunities in Fort Lauderdale.

It didn't take me long to realize how perceptive Bob had been. Fort Lauderdale had a small community of professionals shaping its future. One was a visionary land developer, Jim Hunt, the head of Coral Ridge Properties. He had created the Galt Ocean Mile, among other premium developments. Jim was the first big promoter of expensive land and lots, and though we would not become friends until some years later, I admired him from a distance. I was impressed by his prominence in Fort Lauderdale's business community as well as his strength and ability to manage conditions around him. He was a heavyset man with a strong personality. He later give me some valuable advice as I built my second career in real estate: "Never take both hands off the pump," he said. "As an entrepreneur, you need to be on constant lookout for opportunity, and that will involve risk. But you minimize those risks by keeping one hand on the pump that's producing for you."

But in the summer of 1956, I honestly didn't know what I was going to do with the rest of my life when I moved my family to Fort

Lauderdale. By then, we had the first three of our five sons. We sold our house in Monroe with all the furnishings. Pat sat silently next to me in the front seat of our Lincoln, holding nine-month-old David on her lap. Michael and Tom, ages five and three, played and wrestled and colored in the back. Pat was supportive of our new adventure. Her silence didn't mean she was concerned about our decision to move. Rather, I think it showed her adaptable nature. This makes her not only the best wife in the world, but perhaps the only woman who would ever put up with me. She has always trusted my instincts.

Pat and I moved our family into a rented duplex and enrolled Michael in first grade at Wilton Manors public school. I began reaching out to businessmen in the community and started to search for a suitable lot to build a home on. After I found one, I worked with an architect to design a luxurious model in the $30,000 range, a substantial investment for the time. But before it was completed, a few people offered me almost $40,000 for the property.

I had been used to making $200 and $300 profit on an automobile. Believe me, the offers on our new house got my attention. I was intrigued by the prospect of making almost $10,000 in profit on the sale of a single home. I gave in and began to build a second home in the same price range. Again, I was offered thousands more than I had invested. I sold it and began a third home. This, too, went for a good profit, and I finally realized that a pattern had been established. I had accidentally become a homebuilder.

With Bob Trachsel at my side, I opened Behring Construction Company and moved my parents to Florida. My father went to work for me as a carpenter. We began by building on five lots and selling properties in the $18,000 to $25,000 price range. They went quickly, and I decided to expand. I took in partners to pursue larger projects. We were a hardworking group with a family atmosphere. My father enjoyed getting out with the laborers every day, pounding nails and hanging sheetrock. My mother would make large doughnuts for the crews. In the expansion, I was able to bring more friends down from Wisconsin, including Dan Poff, who had built the apartments in Monroe for me. Dan was an honest and hardworking contractor willing to take a risk. Along with Dan, I convinced Dick Bienema to move south.

It was a good team. Our first major development included 350 units that we turned into waterfront properties by digging canals and building up the land around them. Taking another lesson from Jim Hunt, who could have put P.T. Barnum to shame, I learned to bang the drum loudly. I hired a public relations firm and held major media events to establish the reputation of our homes and land development. Beyond getting a fair markup on the price of a home, the real money came by increasing the value of the land. That was one part vision, one part labor and one part showmanship. The art was in getting others to see its value the way you did. In the beginning, that wasn't easy; much of the land was swampy and had to be dredged and built up. Showmanship attracted investors, and I was soon surrounded by a group of blue-chip partners. We'd split our profits 50-50.

We were also building condominiums, some of the first in the nation. But some of my customers kept telling me that what they really preferred was a single-family home on its own lot with the benefits of condo living—maintenance handled by an association for a fee, community gathering places and more.

So we went to work. We bought 13 acres west of Fort Lauderdale. I named the planned development Tamarac. (The name was similar to the name of a country club I belonged to.) My attorney, Bill Morse, was confident and well connected. He and his wife were big players in state politics. His firm was highly regarded in Tallahassee, the capital. I had hired him to help me with zoning issues and to develop the relatively new concepts of condominiums and land leases. But Bill soon had me involved in politics, supporting candidates like Bud Dickenson, who went on to help establish the Florida Council of 100, a group of business, community and political leaders that I joined.

Bill's firm was helping one candidate for a state senate campaign. In the politics of the old days, I agreed to support him if he would help me in Tallahassee if he won. He did. Once in office, he helped me secure a city charter for Tamarac through the state legislature. It was controversial—we won a charter for 13 acres of raw land. Until then, charters went to communities that were already built out.

This was 1962. On March 3rd of the following year, we held the grand opening of Tamarac, the first city in the United States to offer yard mowing, hedge trimming, exterior painting, roof cleaning and year-round recreational programs with a full-time recreational director as a service of the city. It was a unique concept; it had never been done before. We catered to people 55 and older. Our homes were priced at $8,990 to $12,990. It was a popular concept, and soon we were buying land west of the city, expanding the community, 10,000 acres in all. I controlled the charter, so I made Bill Morse mayor. Today, Tamarac has nearly 70,000 residents.

We based our communities on the idea that retirees wanted a chance to meet and make friends with people like themselves who were moving from their hometowns to Florida. In each area, we constructed 250 homes and a clubhouse, swimming pool, shuffleboard and other recreational amenities. We started many clubhouse activities such as bingo, dancing and barbeques that made each common area a welcome gathering place. Residents no longer needed to worry about outside maintenance, as it was all included in a $23-per-month fee to the city.

It was a big success. *Adult Leisure Living Idea Hits the Jackpot* was the headline in the local paper three years after we broke ground. But it also was one of the first times that I had an inkling of a greater purpose in life. Not only was Tamarac good business, it was something good. We gave people freedom and friendship—at a price they could afford. We created a way of life for them. Now, rather than sitting around in houses waiting to die, retired people could move to Florida to a nice home. They would not have to worry about property maintenance and upkeep and could enjoy a retirement full of fun and activities. In Tamarac, neighborhoods became competitive; residents often approached me to tell me that theirs was the best and most active. And I never raised prices much because I wanted to give this way of life to as many people as possible. It was a lifestyle that was no longer reserved for the wealthy alone.

I got a lot of satisfaction out of it all. I was the "father of the city." I umpired the softball games between neighborhoods. On New Year's Eve, I'd visit every clubhouse to greet the residents. They'd play "Hail to the Chief" when I walked in.

Tamarac's growth brought banks, shopping centers, hospitals, golf courses and everything needed for a comfortable life. Now, more than 40 years later, the original houses are selling for $175,000. The area looks as good today as the day we built it because of the maintenance and the pride residents have in their community.

Pat and I built our home in the Woodlands, an exclusive country club community I developed in Tamarac. It featured two 18-hole championship golf courses designed by Robert Von Hagge and a 58,000-foot clubhouse. Single-family residences ranged from $30,000 to $55,000 in the 640-acre community. It was soon dubbed "Broward's Fashionable West End."

When I turned 40 in 1968, Pat and my friends threw me one heck of a party. The antics were so outrageous that they made the *Miami Herald*. The invitations carried an illustration of me dressed only in a diaper and sitting on top of the world. The cover of the invitation read, "Life begins at 40." The inside copy continued, "Friends of Ken Behring hope to prove this to him." They did that at a rollicking celebration that began at noon and did not end until well into the next day. The bash took place at the Woodlands, where every model home was opened and featured a bar based on a different theme. All homes served barbecued boar, while four bands played continuously for the three or four thousand people who attended the event.

Our financial success in Tamarac was largely due to our purchase of large tracts of land for future development. I had strong people handling land purchased from farmers in the area. Dick Anderson, my marketing manager, sealed a deal for a tract of 1,380 acres that paved the way for the first large expansion of Tamarac. It provided space for a shopping center, golf courses, 1,750 retirement homes and woodlands. It also included a high-end area with two golf courses and expensive villas and homes. Dick was also in charge of selling all commercial land and recreation leases. Chuck Langston, a former baseball player, helped purchase a tract of 5,000 acres that provided the land for the rest of Tamarac. He also found a 3,500-acre tract west of Palm Beach. We built Boca West, a retirement area, there. He also was responsible for our land purchases in St. Petersburg and Lake Tarpon in northwest Florida.

These acquisitions and the increases in the value of our land holdings were the reason we could go public in 1969 and eventually sell the corporation to Cerro Corporation in 1972. As we continued to build Tamarac, we also developed some of the most beautiful and prestigious communities in the state—Royal Palm Isles, Cherry Creek Estates and Gramercy Park in the Coral Ridge Country Club. By 1972, we'd also built hundreds of custom homes and established ourselves as the largest builder in Florida and the 10th largest in the nation.

In Tamarac, Pat blossomed, becoming a community leader in her own right. She joined a number of service organizations, hosting fundraisers and getting actively involved in our children's schools. She was asked to join Beaux Arts, an organization that raised funds for the Fort Lauderdale Museum of Art, and served as chair of the "April in Paris" Easter Lily Ball. She learned how to drive. Pat took on the role of caretaker and provider in the social relationships we enjoyed. She befriended the wives of my partners and served as emotional ambassador to my employees. Everything whirled around us, but Pat was the rock. She held our family together. She made sure we attended the boys' school events and did our part to support community and academic programs.

One successful program we started in Florida was the Behring Outstanding Teacher Award at Pine Crest School, the private school in Fort Lauderdale that our kids attended. We began the program in 1973. It required faculty, administrators and students to vote for three outstanding teachers at the end of the school year. We gave $5,000 to each of those teachers. They were honored at an assembly and featured in the local news. It was an exciting time when the school named the new teachers. But what I found fascinating was that every year the faculty, administrators and students agreed on the winning teachers. It was as if each year, like clockwork, three teachers would distinguish themselves above the rest and be identified unanimously in a private ballot by the three voting blocs. Through the years, Pat has stayed in touch with many of the recipients of the Outstanding Teacher Award. We are proud of their accomplishments and the lives they have powerfully influenced as educators.

I also found purpose in this awards program. The goal was to motivate the best. We feel we did. But we also enjoyed it because we were accomplishing much more for the school than the value of the money we donated to the program. There was purpose to our giving. After the boys graduated from Pine Crest, the Behring Awards ended. But Pat and I established an endowment at the school that provides ongoing grants to teachers for continuing education.

Pine Crest provided our children with strong academic programs and offered them a wonderful environment. David, our third son, excelled in academics and on the football field. At 5 feet, 10 inches and 185 pounds, he became the leading all-time single-season ground gainer in the history of Broward County football, carrying the ball 189 times during the regular season for a total of 1,396 yards. He shattered the old record of 1,246 yards and set individual rushing records in nine games his senior year. In the tenth game, playing on a badly swollen ankle, he led the Pine Crest Panthers to a 6-0 win over Dade Christian by scoring the only touchdown and rushing more than 100 yards. It gave Pine Crest its first undefeated season and district title. Including post-season play that year, David racked up 1,487 yards on 197 carries and scored 12 touchdowns, averaging 7.5 yards per carry.

The fact that I remember these statistics so many years later is a testament to how proud I was of him, as I am of all my sons. Jeff, our fourth son, earned an unprecedented 12 major varsity sports letters. He was a good student and courageously competitive in everything he did. He was by far the most athletic in the family, and we were all envious of his ability to quickly master almost any sport.

As a family, we enjoyed fishing, often traveling into the Arctic Circle to catch trout in the Great Slave and Great Bear Lakes and going after black marlin and sailfish off the coast of Panama. On several occasions, we visited Coiba, a Panamanian prison island. The fishing was great. The waters were home to a submerged island with dozens of different classes of sport fish. In a single day, we caught 28 different varieties. At night, we played volleyball with the inmates and locals, who told us tales of prison life and attempted escapes from the island.

One day, we were fishing in an area inhabited by shark and orca. Jeff lost his grip on the rod as he cast his line. Instinctively, he dove into the shark- and orca-infested water to retrieve the rod and reel. David grabbed him before sharks could attack.

"What are you doing?" he screamed at his wet younger brother. "The sharks could have killed you."

"The sharks or Dad," Jeff answered. "And I figured I had a better chance with the sharks."

It's not that I was a difficult father. But I was as demanding as I was proud. The boys worked hard and played hard at baseball, football, track and tennis. As they grew, each son's unique talents and personalities emerged. They were smart. Michael, our first son, was a gifted artist, with a creative temperament and an interest in music. Tom, our second son, fell in love with books, psychology, philosophy and baseball, and I came to appreciate his thoughtful nature. Perhaps of all the boys, Tom was the most like Pat—a gentle teddy bear, soft-spoken and loved by his nephews and nieces. Scott, our fifth son, was called to the great outdoors and was never one to engage in the conventional life. He played football, lacrosse and wrestled at Pine Crest. Like Tom, he was kind and sensitive, earnest in his relationships and quick to make a friend. In all, the boys were a tribute to Pat and her gift at motherhood. I was a father from the old school, focused on building the business and emotionally distant. My love was demonstrated more than it was expressed. Showing it was, and remains, difficult. I probably inherited that from my father, just as he inherited it from his. It was compounded by the fact that I worked 15-hour days, seven days a week. I am grateful that Pat was—and remains—so supportive of our children.

In January 1969, the *Miami Herald* published a feature article about Pat. It was headlined *She's Gracious Amid Wealth*. The story quotes Pat as saying, "I enjoy the excitement of living with a man who is becoming well-known." The article continues, "That statement is as close as Pat Behring will get to pretentiousness. A woman who describes herself as an introvert, Mrs. Behring is exceedingly gracious. She jumps to offer coffee and her mother-in-law's homemade fruitcake. She realizes instinctively the needs of others, works to put her guests at ease. She succeeds.

"Behring Properties, her husband's company, has an estimated net worth of between $15 and $20 million. But it's people, not money, that matter to Mrs. Behring.

"You have to be tolerant of your husband's time. You have to be willing to share with his business," she said, adding, "When I need him, he's there."

"He's the head of the home, although the responsibility for everyday things falls on me…. I don't think I could ever find a more exciting man."

Pat was, and continues to be, gracious. The Herald story may appear dated in relation to today's attitudes, but there's no question that her support provided the foundation I needed to build our career. Business did not end at the front door, and Pat never hesitated to help me in whatever venture I was pursuing. Our Woodlands home was filled with guests and galas and even historic press conferences.

One of most exciting press events was with the legendary entertainer Jackie Gleason. I met Gleason through a friend. Bob von Hagge worked with Gleason on golf courses. Bob suggested I hire Gleason's Miami public relations man. Soon I had met Jackie and we were in business together.

Gleason and I planned to build the most magnificent golf courses in the world on a major development, with luxury homes. The centerpiece of the six-course complex, to be designed by Bob, would be a 7,300-yard championship course known as "The Great One." We planned to host a Professional Golfers' Association event there, "Nonpareil"—at $300,000, the richest cup on the tour. Our plans included a three-tiered stadium and room for 100,000 spectators on the course. Permanent television towers on each hole would provide perfect network coverage for all tournaments.

We announced the project in 1969. According to Jackie, it even had the blessing of President Richard Nixon. Attending the media event were Colin Brown, president and chairman of National Gypsum; his vice president of corporate affairs, William Duncan; Judge John P. Lomenzo, a good friend of mine and secretary of state of New York; executives from 3M; and Bob von Hagge and his wife,

Greta, one of the beautiful June Taylor dancers, who opened Gleason's show every week with his signature "And away we go!"

"We will not be topped!" The Great One bellowed to the press. "If someone offers to match or beat our purse, we will up the ante so that the 'Nonpareil' will be the richest tourney in history. I've found plenty of men with great ideas and with guts, but never before have I found one who also has the cabbage," he said, complimenting me. He then told reporters that the first tournament was already in planning, with 3M as the sponsor. His network, CBS, would broadcast the five-day event, he said.

Not only was Gleason "The Great One," he was also the great improviser. He held court in our home, painting a vivid picture of the future. I stood next to him, nervously calculating the time and money involved in the venture, not to mention the cost of working with Jackie Gleason, who had only one way of doing things—his way. The project would cost more than half a billion dollars. It would cover 5,000 acres of prime land between Fort Lauderdale and Pompano Beach. It would require zoning, architectural designs, new roads and the creation of an island inaccessible to automobile traffic, where Jackie intended to have his palace overlooking the 9th, 16th, 17th and 18th holes. It would require us to move a million and a half cubic yards of earth. And here he was, not only locking down the television rights of the first tournament, but committing that the project would be completed by the end of the following year.

And away we go.

In the end, Gleason and I went our separate ways. We realized we wouldn't be able to complete the project. In the best of show business terms, you could say that we had "creative differences." Jackie wanted a showcase for his home, his talent and his life lived large in every sense of the term. I simply wanted to make money. It was not long before we realized that we could not have it both ways. We quietly dropped the venture six months after the press conference.

My baby picture, 1928

*My parents, Elmer and
Mae Behring, in the 1920s.
The stern expressions were
typical of their Swiss-
German heritage.*

Boy Scout Behring, Troop 114, Monroe, Wisconsin, about 1939. Still a little thin for football.

Me at age 18, captain of the high school football team. Below, a ticket to a game, like the ones I used to leave on the kitchen table for my parents.

Monroe

High School

FOOTBALL

ADULT TICKET

Adm. 33c, tax 7c
Total 40c

The Cheesemakers of Monroe High School, 1945. I've got the ball.

High school graduation pictures for me and Pat, 1946.

Cutting the cake at our wedding in 1949

One of my first cars, a 1939 Buick Century. My passion for cars was well developed by the time of this picture.

After I started my own used cars lot, I went into business with my father-in-law, Budd Riffle.

The house I grew up in.

My first car dealership, Lincoln-Mercury.

I am in business as a homebuilder in Florida, 1957. My first three sons, Tom, David, and Michael.

Our first house in Florida—I built it.

Pat and I relaxing at our house in "The Woodlands" in Tamarac.

Jackie Gleason and me at a press conference at our Woodlands home, 1969.

Our Modiflex factory in Tamarac.

Honoring teachers at a party at our kids' school, Pine Crest, 1974.

Umpiring at a baseball game at Tamarac. The glasses helped me call the pitches.

Party invitation—
Life begins at 40, 1968.

Meeting the Tamarac residents at a barbeque.

The boys in Florida, 1962: Jeff, Tom holding Scott, Michael and David.

The boys grown up— Jeff, David, Scott, Tom and Michael.

David Behring, #32, playing football for Pine Crest School.

*In the Seahawks locker
room at the Kingdome
in Seattle.*

*On the sidelines for
a Seahawks game.*

*Carrying the ball at
the headquarters of
the Seattle Seahawks.*

The Blackhawk ranch, soon to become a community.

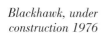

Blackhawk, under construction 1976

Hitting the links with my good friend, Ken Hofmann.

A marlin, more than 1,000 lbs., I caught in Australia

A 21-foot, 3500 lb. crocodile I took in Tanzania.

A 12-point elk I took in Colorado.

My first classic car, a 1937 Cord Sportsman.

Jay Leno, a classic car lover, joins Pat and I at the opening of our car museum.

I received an honorary doctorate from Brigham Young University in 2002.

Opening the Principal Leadership Institute at the University of California, Berkeley, 2000.

Opening of "The American Presidency" exhibit with the Smithsonian Institute.

*With my good friend,
King Juan Carlos of
Spain.*

*Pat and I with former
President Bush.*

*With former President
Clinton on my plane.*

'03 5 15

Unlike Gleason, I was pragmatic about land development and the construction business. I had weathered economic slumps and worked through labor shortages. I'd seen my business turned upside down by price spikes in building materials. I'd suffered attacks from politicians trying to make an issue out of zoning ordinances and land leases. Through it all, I had proved that I could make things work. I could stand up to Gleason and his desire to build an adult Disney World. We parted as friends. Besides, I had become interested in factory-produced housing, and that began to take more of my time.

We had a problem in the building business. In 1968, lumber prices rose 33 percent, particularly for plywood and softwood framing lumber. National housing starts were projected to hit 1.5 million that year, far short of need. The industry was plagued by a shortage of qualified craftsman. Florida was in a recession. The solution to these challenges, I believed, was steel-framed factory-built homes. Mine would be as beautiful as traditional homes, but they could be built in a factory and assembled on a lot in three pieces at a much lower cost. Total assembly time would be one hour.

I still believe it was a good idea. We'd be able to build houses in much higher quantities to meet demand. We'd get around labor problems to stabilize the costs of building. And we'd standardize everything, with the exception of consumer preferences in colors, façade, models and amenities.

I took time to educate myself on the prefabricated housing market. I learned that that no one was producing a quality product. I assembled a team to meet the challenge I presented: build a perfect home that could be mass-produced in a controlled factory environment and assembled quickly but permanently on a lot, while providing all the beauty and options available in traditional construction. I asked Bill Brangham, my executive vice president at the Behring Corporation, to lead the group. Bill was gifted at sales and marketing and possessed good insight into consumer attitudes.

George Smith, vice president of Behring Properties, oversaw the engineering and materials management. I had hired him away from General Electric (GE) along with several other GE alumni. Working with John Evans, our project architect, and Evan Morton, project engineer, George put together the infrastructure blueprint for what we called Modiflex Homes. The venture grabbed media attention from the day we announced it in May 1969.

We constructed the first prototype on a lot in Tamarac. It generated so much interest that we had to build a wall to keep people out. Some of them were coming from outside the country to see what we were doing. Top materials and steel frames made our homes more durable than traditional wood homes. To make them attractive, we developed five different models. Each could be assembled in three pieces on a prepoured concrete foundation with plumbing and electrical hookups. We transported each one from factory to lot on three flatbed trailers. One truck would carry the bedroom wing; another, the living room section; and the third a wet wing, containing bathrooms, utility room, kitchen and dining room. Each section would be hoisted from the flatbed by a giant crane and bolted to the foundation by cast-in-steel inserts. When the sections were in place and fastened to each other with steel bolts, the roof would be lowered into position and workmen would connect the plumbing and electricity.

Along with the five models, we offered over 150 variations on the exterior. At the end of assembly, a Modiflex Home—though less expensive to build and more durable in construction—would look no different from a traditional home next door. With assembly-line efficiency, we could sell units and lots from $12,000 to $17,000 and promise buyers that they could be in their new homes within a week. Convinced of our vision, we built the factory in Tamarac. It was a 250,000-square-foot facility that cost more than $4 million.

The venture created international buzz. Government officials, economists, industrialists and builders came from as far away as

Japan to tour our facility. Many observers were interested in joint venturing with us to build Modiflex Homes in their countries. We set up an educational center to meet the demands of the curious, with maps, color photographs, diagrams and models. In a three-month period, we had more than 250,000 visitors. Even the Shah of Iran sent a representative to learn about what we were doing.

The timing was right. In Washington, Congress was calling for solutions to the housing shortage. In a speech, Sen. Harrison A. Williams, a member of the Senate Housing Committee, challenged Americans to "devote the same energy and talent that enabled us to win the race to the moon to home building." Speaking to the National Housing Center Council, which was made up of manufacturer members of the National Association of Home Builders, Williams said, "In recent years, there has been much rhetoric about a missile gap or space gap followed by huge expenditures for our military and space programs.... It's time we focused our attention on the housing gap." Earlier, the Commerce Department had predicted that within a few years, the United States would lag far behind other countries in housing its people. It said that the best-housed people in the world would be living in the Soviet Union.

Sen. Williams quoted the department and said, "If a Pentagon general said the same thing about missiles, there would be an enormous clamor for a multi-billion-dollar crash program.... It is a national disgrace that the United States is falling far behind other nations in providing better housing. Last year, the United States built 7.69 new housing units per 1,000 residents. By way of contrast, Sweden built 13.43 units per 1,000, Japan built 11.89, the Soviet Union built 9.80, the Netherlands built 9.63 and France built 8.32."

For a while, it appeared not only that we had met the marketing needs of consumers, but that we were onto something of tremendous importance to American public policy. We offered an attractive, efficient and cost-effective answer to meeting the nation's growing housing needs. One popular magazine put a Modiflex Home on its cover and proclaimed, "Assembly Line Homes: An Important New Trend in Housing." My small company had grown from a handful of close friends to more than 700 employees.

Another magazine wrote that the ideas coming from the Behring Corporation were the "fountainhead of most significant developments." Whether intentional or not, the reference to the book by libertarian economist and philosopher Ayn Rand would prove fitting for Modiflex Homes. Rand's book is about a visionary architect who creates revolutionary buildings that solve serious social problems. But his work is undone by government bureaucracies, unions, rivals and traditionalists. It was the perfect metaphor for our new company. As word spread about the popularity of Modiflex Homes, so did opposition.

First, the carpenters' union came out against us. It suggested that Modiflex Homes would undermine the security of its members and even destroy its organization. That didn't deter us. We were using highly skilled labor in our factory and could weather the challenge. But soon, the union solicited and gained support from the Teamsters union, a group that could not be broken. Suddenly, truckers would not transport our homes from factory to lot. Next, our opponents launched a major lobbying effort against us in state legislatures and city halls. What we were doing, they charged, was risky. We were challenging conventional thinking and the long history of traditional homebuilding, perhaps even undermining the economy. Under pressure from special interest groups, cities and towns began delaying and even denying zoning for our homes. Soon it began to taking us longer to get a government permit than to build the home. New battles emerged every day.

In *The Fountainhead*, the hero/architect retreats in the end and destroys his visionary creations. I was determined to press forward.

But we had miscalculated. Suddenly, our best workers began leaving the factory. They could earn $2 an hour more in construction jobs in the field. Hoping to keep our costs down, I had talked the union into working for us for a rate that now appeared too low. I had not anticipated the possible consequences. When I offered to increase workers' wages, their union said, "No way. That's the rate you wanted. That's the rate you get." The union's goal was to protect its members working on construction sites. Before long, I could not recruit the quality people who could do the job right. I learned a valuable lesson.

The apparent solution to our problem came from the outside. With the success of the homebuilding business, our land leases and our holdings in Tamarac (including shopping centers, recreational and maintenance contracts, increasingly valuable property and a city charter itself), several large companies were interested in acquiring the Behring Corporation. I began to consider offers seriously. I was intrigued by the possibility that for the first time in my life, I wouldn't have to worry about money or managing anything. No more juggling payroll and payables, keeping my company together on perception and the good fortune of not having banks call my loans. I could see freedom, but I was also worried about what would come next if I sold out.

Still, companies willing to pay me more than I ever imagined were courting me. My team and I had created something of value, and I felt good about that. I entertained offers from Bethlehem Steel, Dupont, Chrysler and National Gypsum. The closest I came to selling was entering a tentative deal with National Gypsum for $30 million in stock. However, it required me to stay and help run the company I was selling. And when I traveled to the corporation's headquarters in upstate New York, I was shocked. There were layers of management, emotionless bureaucrats, countless meetings—all of the things I dreaded about big business. I considered calling off the deal.

By this time, Jim Hunt had become a good friend. He was the godfather of land development and property management in Fort

Lauderdale. He had become something of a mentor, first telling me never to take both hands off the pump, then teaching me by example how to create buzz to promote sales and increase the value of land.

As I struggling with my decision, he shared with me his regret for having sold his beloved Coral Ridge Properties to Westinghouse Corporation two years earlier. Not long after the transaction, he invited me to lunch. Sitting across the table as glum as Woody Allen, he expressed his unhappiness. "They made me rich," he said. "And I have an office. But it has bars around it. Every once in a while, they come in with a stick and poke me to see if I'll growl." Once supreme ruler of his own domain, Jim had been stripped of his motivation. He made it clear to me that the measure of success in business sometimes has little to do with making money. "Everything is run by committee," he told me. "No one takes risks. The emotion is gone." Westinghouse had even installed the man who served as Jim's number two at Coral Ridge Properties as Jim's boss.

I took his advice to heart. I told National Gypsum I would not enter into a formal contract. Instead, I took the greater risk and asked the Oppenheimer Company on Wall Street to take me public. Working with a couple of bright young advisors, including Tom Seward and Henry Silverman, we merged 6 of the 30-plus companies I owned—including Modiflex Homes, the city charter of Tamarac, land and my home-building business—into one company to be listed on the American Stock Exchange. We sold a million shares at $16.50 a share. I retained about five million shares. In the first few days of trading, the stock shot up to $30 a share. That amount of money and my sudden wealth—I was worth $150 million on paper—was almost inconceivable to me.

My mother, thankfully, was around to keep me grounded. I had given her shares in my company before the public offering. Her question to me was, "What am I supposed to do with them?"

"You keep them," I answered. "And after the company goes public and the value of the shares increase, you sell them."

"Why?"

"To make money."

"How do I make money?"

"By selling the shares."

"What do I have to do?" Her question was filled with suspicion.

I answered as simply as I could. "You just have to sell the shares."

"Do I have to attend meetings?"

"No."

"Do I have to do anything for anyone?"

"No, you hold the shares and then sell them."

"And they give me the money, just like that?"

"Exactly."

She slid the stock certificate back across my desk. "Doesn't seem right."

Despite the opportunities and money I provided them, my parents refused to spend what I gave them to enjoy the finer things in life. After they were gone, I found thousands of dollars hidden in their mattresses—along with my football clippings. I wish I had known they saved those clippings when they were alive. If only my parents had been able to share them with me, I would have known how much they really cared.

As for my newfound wealth, I now had a large bank account. But before long, that would not be enough for me—again.

Chapter 5:
A PLACE CALLED BLACKHAWK

Far better to dare mighty things, to win glorious triumphs, even though checkered by failure, than to rank with those poor spirits who neither enjoy much, nor suffer much because they live in the great twilight that knows not victory nor defeat.

Theodore Roosevelt

If there's a pattern to my life, it's that I do something new about every 10 years. In the 1950s, it was the automobile business. In the 1960s, I developed land in Florida. By the end of that decade, I was manufacturing preconstructed homes.

The activities of one period always overlapped. But one cycle was becoming certain: about every decade, I would become restless and need to make a major change in my life. I believe every life comes with the possibility of great adventure and that new pursuits will keep the adventure alive, the mind sharp and boredom at bay. I sometimes follow one opportunity to another, but I often set out to make a wholesale change—a new environment, a new purpose, new discoveries and new friends.

That was the case in 1972.

I sold my company that year to Cerro Corporation, a major copper company that was diversifying and owned Leadership Housing, the division that would run the Behring Corporation. After the deal, I had about $50 million in net worth. I had decided I didn't like running a public company after all. I didn't like the restrictions that came with being public, such as government filings and constant reports to shareholders. My 10 years was up again, this time with the building business in Florida. With the sale of my company, I had achieved the American Dream. But where to go and what to do next?

I decided to take a month off to think about it. I planned to take my family and mother to Europe for a needed rest. I wanted to reward everyone for putting up with me while I was under the pressure of selling my company. My mother helped ease the pressure with a funny, but typical, incident.

I sent the family ahead to Switzerland as I went to New York to finish some business. I always stayed at the Waldorf Towers. My mother met me there. My secretary accompanied her to New York and was to bring my mother up to my suite on the 30th floor. She had never been in an elevator; she refused to enter it, saying she would walk up 30 stories. I rode down to the lobby and pulled her into the elevator. She held her hands over her eyes on the way up.

It was evening and we were flying to Switzerland the following day. I had to leave early for a meeting, so I asked her what she wanted for breakfast the next morning. I told her it would be brought to her room. She said she wanted coffee, eggs, bacon and toast.

The next day, when I returned to the hotel after my meetings, the bellman told me there had been a problem. Apparently, when room service delivered my mother her breakfast, she had refused to sign for it. "I am not going to let you rob my son!" she told the waiter.

"All you had to do is sign," I told her. "You didn't have to pay."

"I could not eat food that expensive," she said.

After we returned from Europe, I began to explore new possibilities. I traveled to Asia to consult and look at some of the dynamic growth occurring in the Pacific Rim. One morning in Tokyo, the phone rang in my hotel room. It was Bruce Devlin, a golf course architect I had worked with in Florida to build 10 courses. He was calling from the States. Even with the phone connection fading in and out, I could hear excitement in Bruce's voice.

"On your way back to Florida, you need to stop in California," Bruce said. "I think there's something here you'll be interested to see."

"What do you have?" I asked.

"I don't want to tell you over the telephone. I want you to see it for yourself."

I trusted Bruce. He knew how to spot an opportunity, and I was interested. I stopped in San Francisco on my return from Japan. Bruce met me at the airport, and we jumped into a chartered helicopter. It took us north from San Francisco, over Oakland, and out beyond majestic Mount Diablo. The land beneath us was barren but beautiful. It had rolling hills and long valleys, scattered ranches, walnut groves and desert brush.

I nodded at Bruce inside the helicopter. He was right. The property had potential. From the air, it was clear that development was moving in this direction. One subdivision had already been completed near the area; roads were being paved in other places in anticipation of future development.

"It's called Blackhawk Ranch," Bruce shouted above the noise of the rotors. "About 5,000 acres."

"I'm surprised it's available," I answered, looking down at a large round barn and well-maintained horse ranch.

"Named after a famous racehorse," Bruce shouted again.

"I'm surprised it's available," I repeated.

"Only recently. Developers had it, but the operation went bankrupt. A dealer in heavy construction machinery bought it, built a home and just put the rest of the property back on the market."

As we continued to fly over the land, I imagined what it could look like: a couple of groomed golf courses, surrounded by homes, trees and retail property. We could develop a number of communities, similar to what we had done at the Woodlands in Florida. And there was potential for future expansion.

"It could be a medium- to high-end development," I said to Bruce. "We could probably put 5,000 single-family homes down there." I was enthusiastic but cautious.

"You like it?" Bruce asked.

"I want Bob to see this and hear what he thinks," I said. Bruce nodded. After flying over the property several more times, we returned to the airport.

Bob Carrau was a California homebuilder working for Leadership Housing, a division of Cerro. I liked him from the moment we had met during Cerro's purchase of my company. More important, I trusted his decisions, particularly since Leadership Housing had become successful in California and recently expanded into Florida. I contacted Bob and joined him to look at the site. He saw its possibilities as well.

"I'd take it all," he said.

I told him I wasn't interested in that, particularly because the owner had recently built a huge house on the property. He would sell it only if a buyer met his outrageous price. "I'm interested in maybe 4,000 acres," I said. "I see 4,000 acres with tremendous potential."

Bob agreed. "I don't think you can lose," he said. Bob offered to help develop the land and the property if I made him a partner.

I was still living in Florida and had not considered moving to California. I would need someone of Bob's experience on the ground to see the project through, and his offer further confirmed our hopes. So did his willingness to leave Leadership and join me in the venture. Beyond this, I knew how difficult the California development process was. It included strong environmental protections. Bob's participation would be invaluable. I welcomed him as a partner and proceeded to buy the land. I acquired 4,000 acres for $4 million. I put down $400,000 and got the best 400 acres released for immediate development. I negotiated a 10-year note at 4 percent in 10 equal payments. Additional land would be released as I paid for it.

From my perspective, the arrangement was a no-lose deal. I soon realized just how important the terms would be to the success of the project. Though we had not discussed it in detail, Bob knew that developing Blackhawk would come with serious challenges, particularly from an environmental standpoint. The environmental law and approval process gave activists power against any major development. Their strategy was simple, and at the time was actually being taught as a formal course at the University of California, Berkeley. It was to intimidate county supervisors into limiting or rejecting a project and tie up development with lawsuits. Each suit forced a delay. After so many delays, developers could no longer afford to have their money tied up and unproductive. The cost of delays would become too high, and developers would either have to surrender, go bankrupt, or both.

Fortunately for us, the terms I structured with the seller did not tie up a lot of cash and allowed my team to fight back from a position of strength. That's what we did, as small threats from our opponents turned into what the media would come to call the Blackhawk Wars. Bob Carrau brought in a young hard-nosed attorney from Walnut Creek with remarkable attention to detail. His name was Dan VanVoorhis. He specialized in zoning and appeared to thrive in a hot political environment. The hotter the environment, the better he performed. He could out-analyze and out-talk anyone.

Our strategy was to ask for as much as possible from the very beginning—to start so big that after the other side pushed back, we'd still come out ahead. Our initial design was for a country club with two golf courses surrounded by 5,000 homes. It would be the biggest development ever planned for Northern California.

"You go that big and you're going to attract attention," someone warned. "I'd start out smaller."

"We're going to attract attention anyway," Dan said. "This way, if they cut us back, we still win."

They did try to cut. A group of local residents joined The Sierra Club and an organization named "Save Mt. Diablo." They created a misleading picture of homes being constructed on the top of Mt. Diablo. (We could not build there and did not want to. Much of the mountain was part of a state park.) The coalition circulated a petition and within 30 days collected 33,000 signatures against us—despite that fact that our development would be miles from the summit of the mountain and did not even interfere with Mount Diablo State Park. Their efforts were also energized by a broad-based campaign against the Walt Disney Company, which had proposed building a winter resort near Lake Tahoe. Every step we took would be met with a lawsuit, and the fight became so high profile that the Sierra Club turned it into a fundraising opportunity.

Two activists led the fight against us. They were taking the Berkeley course and getting credit for their campaign. Their work was front-page news in the Contra Costa Times. Although both Dan and I refused to be intimidated, their stalling tactics were successful in delaying the project. After a few years, I believed the price of the property would never decrease and that I would eventually develop the land. So I purchased the site outright and put part of the land in trust for my children. Bob Carrau felt that he had taken the project as far as he could and was ready for a change.

I agreed that we needed a new team to move forward. During Christmas dinner in 1974, I approached Steve Beinke and Owen Schwaderer, members of my Florida organization. They thrived on hard work and were steadfast in their loyalty. Steve in his twenties and Owen in his early thirties, they were the youngest members of our group. They had distinguished themselves on a number of projects, including converting apartments to condominiums. With wives and children, they were eager to build a future with me in California. They would come to the state and join my former Florida attorney, Bill Morse.

As 1975 began, the new team went to work building positive relations with the county government. We understood the problems faced by our local officials, particularly having to deal with petitions opposing the project. We decided to address the situation in a practical way. Our strategy was to give the politicians victories that they could take back to their constituents. One of them was to gift 2,800 acres back to the government to enlarge Mount Diablo State Park and put a buffer between our development and the mountain. We would build on the remaining 1,200 acres that were best suited for homes. We also offered to cut the development to 2,500 homes, half of what we had proposed initially.

Five years after we had bought the land, our strategy finally paid off. By asking for everything, we received something, and that was enough to win approval of the project. Rather than build 5,000 high- and middle-income homes, we would build fewer. We'd make all the homes high end so they'd sell only to wealthy professionals. So, in the end, we won, the environmentalists won and the county and state governments won. In fact, the only unfortunate part was that middle-class consumers could have benefited from our initial plan. We broke ground in June 1977.

Today, I believe the Blackhawk Wars succeeded in making the development one of the best in America. After we began building the high-end homes, I also won approval to build several middle-class communities in the area, particularly as we improved Crow Canyon Road leading into Blackhawk. While we were upgrading the road, I optioned some adjoining land at the unprecedented price of $10,000 an acre and later got permission to build 5,000 units there. Chevron and Pacific Bell were moving employees into two large office buildings in the area. We built homes for their executives and apartments for their workers. The development, called Canyon Lakes, would eventually include 4,500 homes and a public golf course. It was completed in three years and made more money than Blackhawk. But our Blackhawk negotiations helped streamline the process. Later, I would build two developments on the other side of Mount Diablo, retirement communities similar to Tamarac.

Blackhawk would become my signature development and eventually my home. I constructed a 30,000-square-foot house there overlooking the country club. The idea of creating lifestyle-oriented communities became hugely popular in California, particularly for professionals in San Francisco and Oakland. They wanted more open space and larger homes in secluded and secure areas, and a sense of belonging.

The vision I had of the golf course and surrounding homes in the helicopter ride was finally becoming reality. Our team made certain the community was elegant in every detail. We controlled the architecture and color of every home built, as well as the landscaping and management of the two golf courses. A firm believer in advertising and public relations, I tied up the front page of the real estate sections of the San Francisco Examiner and the San Francisco Chronicle for an entire year. The marketing blitz created such a buzz that Blackhawk quickly sold out. The demand was so high that some of the lots that initially cost me $1,000 an acre are valued at more than $2 million today. This was a boon for my five sons, who owned some of the property in trust. It made them all multimillionaires. The fame of Blackhawk has spread around the world. Developers as far away as China named their own communities after ours and asked for my help in trying to duplicate its success.

Most of the homes in Blackhawk have more than doubled in value. Even some people who fought us in the Blackhawk Wars have moved into the community. They now realize what can be done with

land if it's developed properly. Along with moving tons of earth to
build golf courses, lots for homes and beautiful water areas, we
planted more than 400,000 trees. Today these trees have matured.
They are beautiful.

We were able to succeed because of the team we put together.
Despite long periods of frustration and doubts, we never lost sight of
what we wanted to create. I was clearly invested in the project. At
one point, I owned all of the land. There was no way to develop it
unless Blackhawk moved forward. The others were motivated by the
battle and the possibilities of what Blackhawk could become. They
were able to look beyond where we were at any given moment and
stay focused on where we were going.

Blackhawk was going to be something special, and if the county
government gave us the opportunity, we would prove it. Doug Dahlin
was an invaluable member of our California group; he is one of the
most gifted architects I know. He helped me bring to life what I had
pictured during that helicopter ride. He captured my vision and
improved it with his own talent in designing the community and
styles of the homes, down to their interiors. That was key: to have
each member of our team express his respective genius in the
details. Good thing for me—I am not a detail person. I don't have the
patience to get down into the weeds. The dynamic of Steve, Owen,
Dan and Doug balanced perfectly with my vision. We were able to
inspire and motivate one another, even during the darkest days of the
Blackhawk Wars.

Recently, I asked Steve Beinke what he believed was the most
important lesson we learned from the Blackhawk Wars. Without
hesitation, he answered, the need to be sincerely involved in the
community, to immerse ourselves so people come to know and trust
us. We began winning the Blackhawk Wars when we began listening
to the concerns of others and letting them know that we understood
how they felt and were willing to address their needs. We began

winning when we looked at the situation from the point of view of the local community and of county leaders who had to make decisions to satisfy all constituencies.

"Nothing is more important than working directly with the people," Steve said. "You can't simply hire consultants, make a plan and say, 'This is it.' That won't work anymore, especially in sensitive areas like California, Florida and the Northwest. Large projects cannot proceed in these areas anymore without the developers being a part of the community, trusted and known to put the interests of the community ahead of their own."

Steve is right. Blackhawk taught us—as I have learned many other times through the years—that there is no substitute for credibility and goodwill. In any endeavor they provide the foundation for success.

Part III

Different

Chapter 6:
FROM BLACKHAWK TO THE SEAHAWKS

When one door closes, another opens.

Alexander Graham Bell

In 1988, I did something that many American boys dream about: I bought a professional football team, the Seattle Seahawks. That was different, for certain. The team was an expansion organization that had seen its share of ups and downs in its few years of existence.

The Nordstrom family owned it. The Nordstroms were good friends, particularly the late Jim Nordstrom, one of the most honorable businessmen I've ever known. And Seattle is a wonderful city. There are many diehard Seahawks fans. A large and active press corps followed the sport. But the team had yet to catch fire the way other franchises had, especially in larger markets. I felt we could do a lot to build the program. I was up to the challenge. Most important, the purchase worked on a business level.

Jim Nordstrom was one of the best salesmen in the world—just look at the success of his family's chain of department stores. I thought I'd learned something about the art after 30 years in sales myself. But Jim Nordstrom took me back to school. He had invited me to Washington State to discuss business unrelated to football. Unknown to me, his family had decided to sell the Seahawks. Some members wanted to get out of football to concentrate on retailing. It was no coincidence, then, that on the way back to the airport for my return flight to Northern California, Jim asked if I wouldn't mind making a detour.

We ended up at the Seahawks' practice field. Within a few minutes, all my memories of high school football came rushing back. Jim introduced me to players who were quickly becoming legends—stars like Steve Largent and Brian Bosworth—and the coaches under the leadership of Chuck Knox. The experience was larger than life. I guess enthusiasm showed in my eyes. Jim didn't waste any time; he said he was looking for a buyer for the team. We briefly discussed price, and by the time I arrived at the airport to catch my flight, we had shaken hands.

I paid $79 million for the Seahawks. I owned a majority of the team. My friend Ken Hofmann, a California developer who is one of the owners of the Oakland A's baseball franchise, came in for 25 percent. Steve Beinke of my company bought 6 percent and a few other close friends purchased 1 percent each. Part of my motivation—and the reason I was able to make a quick decision—was that the purchase worked for me on a tax level. It provided me with an opportunity to take some of my ordinary income, taxed at higher rates, and shelter it with the depreciation charges of player salaries. But I couldn't hide my excitement when I spoke with my son David after I returned to California. I knew that if anyone could share how I felt, it would be he. He had not only been a standout player in high school but was one of the most devoted fans of professional football I knew.

After the Nordstroms announced the sale, I went to Seattle for a press conference. There was a lot of publicity, both in the newspapers and on TV. I became an instant celebrity. Suddenly, I was famous. When I walked down the street, everyone would point or look at me. It was much different from being a builder. Whenever there was a game, fans would stop me on the way into the stadium. Eventually, I needed a police escort to get up to the owner's box at the stadium, which was called the Kingdome. I grew to enjoy it. My box seated 40 guests. I loved asking friends and celebrities to join me. We always had good food and the best seats in the house. I enjoyed football so much that I started standing on the sidelines with the players. You could feel the intensity of the game. If you won, the locker room afterward was the highlight of the night. If you lost, you immediately went home. There was a famous bar and restaurant near the stadium, McCrory's, where everyone went when the game ended. After victories, it was crowded and I was the celebrity of the moment.

Owning the Seahawks actually delighted the entire family. Two of my sons became involved in the organization, and we attended the games as a group. We often flew to Seattle on a DC-9 I had purchased as a corporate jet. The fans welcomed us, and it appeared that the future was bright. We finished my first season as owner with a 9-7 record, the best ever for the Seahawks. We had won the challenging AFC West division and lost a first-round playoff game to Cincinnati in a heartbreaker. The Seahawks had never won a division title before.

For a while, it appeared that the sky was the limit. It was a pleasure to work with the local community and speak to business and civic organizations. The fans were optimistic about the future. I enjoyed being around them and being part of the energy of the National Football League. At that time, there were only 28 teams in the NFL. It was an exclusive club. The owners included many of the household names that had built the league. They were great men from great families. They were motivated more by their desire to make professional football the most popular sport in the world than by personal greed. It was as much a mission as it was a profession. To be around them—and be associated with the greatest athletes in the world—seemed like a dream.

I enjoyed Seattle and decided to move there. We bought a home on an island, near the Nordstrom family. I also purchased a condominium close to the team offices and spent as much time as I could there and with fans. I had learned a hard lesson from jumping into Modiflex Homes before I fully understood the industry, so I was determined to keep the decision-making for the team with the people who had the expertise. That meant the general manager, the coaches and the scouts. I took a deliberate hands-off approach. I limited my involvement to sitting with my family and friends in the owner's box of the Kingdome and attending the owners' meetings.

But after we finished the following season at 8-8, I felt my management style needed some changes. From my perspective, there were several problems. Many of our draft selections did not pan out. Our conditioning program had room for improvement. And our team was not making enough revenue to land top talent. I watched, frustrated, as top players went to teams in larger markets with more lucrative stadium deals. We had some of the finest linemen in the league, but we lacked a quarterback who could make things happen. And our running backs were not strong enough to balance our offensive attack. For a while, the team appeared one-dimensional, relying heavily on Steve Largent, our star receiver, to carry the team. That was not going to get us where we wanted to be—a divisional powerhouse with a playoff victory or two en route to an eventual Super Bowl.

Tom Flores, a top coach, had been a friend for some time. He had proven himself a winner with the 1981 World Champion Oakland Raiders and the 1984 World Champion L.A. Raiders. I offered him total freedom if he would come in as general manager and work with Chuck Knox to build us a top team. He agreed and took over operations. Again, I stepped back and waited for his assessment. It came loud and clear after the 1990 season, which ended with a disappointing 7-8. Tom felt that if he was going to be responsible for turning the team around, he also needed to take over as head coach. We discussed the idea seriously. I liked Chuck Knox. He was a player's coach, with one of the best records in the league. But I could not honestly say that he was getting everything he needed to produce the kind of winning team I wanted.

A long-term lease between the Seahawks and King County, owner of the Kingdome, was hurting our ability to develop the franchise. The economics weren't working. Teams shared television revenue equally and split ticket sales revenue 60/40 (60% for the home team, 40% for the visiting team). But stronger teams had stadium agreements that also let them raise working capital through concession sales, skyboxes, club seating, parking and advertising. We had almost none of that in the Kingdome. The stadium was small, with only a few skyboxes shared between us, the baseball team and Kingdome. When we asked the county to renegotiate our lease, it wouldn't budge. So I didn't have many alternatives. I believed Chuck was doing the best he could with what he had, but I also needed to give Tom the authority to do what was necessary to create a winning team. With that, I removed Chuck and made Tom general manager, president and head coach. He took charge of our recruiting, and we signed a few players who gave us reason to hope.

Unfortunately, our conditioning program was still weak. Our players were not in top shape. As in the previous two seasons, we lost a handful of games in the final minutes and by only a few points—a sure sign of conditioning troubles. But things went from bad to worse. That season, 26 of our players, including six linebackers, were out with injuries. The situation had deteriorated so much that by the end of the season, we were literally hiring players only days before a game. The consequences were devastating. We ended the season 2-14. The press ripped into me. Many of the attacks were personal; I was referred to a "Bubba" or "Bozo," and the "wealthy California developer" tag, never popular in Seattle, caused more resentment than ever. I tried not to think about them, but they troubled me, particularly because they upset my family.

From the day I bought the team, my son David had been an asset to me. He had studied the team and game closely. From the beginning, he was unofficially involved in the decision-making. He had studied the scouting reports and participated in the drafts. He had learned the front office and taken the time to reach out to the community. He also had attended the owners' meetings with me and built friendships with sons of other owners who were stepping into important roles within the league. I talked to Tom about stepping aside as president and putting David in that position. I told Tom I was concerned that having one man wear three vital hats diluted his focus and ability to function at his best. Most NFL teams have had similar experiences when the head coach was given this much responsibility.

It was not an easy discussion. Tom realized that a head coach who serves as president is often conflicted and unable to work properly with his athletes. For example, a coach who is trying to persuade a recruit to play for him while at the same time negotiating that player's salary is in a tough position. So is a coach who is forced to worry about gate receipts, community outreach and promotional events.

We all realized what needed to be done, and in December 1992, I named David president of the Seahawks organization. I was proud of him and the way he worked. He kept the front office intact and developed a healthy relationship with Tom. His first priority was to sit down with the team physicians and determine what had happened to our players. Twenty-six injuries was not normal or acceptable. Clearly, we needed to change our conditioning program. David made those changes. He also went to work with the media and fans to repair relationships that had been deteriorating. He worked with other NFL owners to understand the coming changes in the league, including the salary cap, which was initiated in his first year.

That year, the team came back with a 6-10 record. Again, it could have been better, but some factors were out of our control. For example, David successfully acquired two prime free agents— offensive lineman Howard "House" Ballard and two-time All Pro cornerback Nate Odomes. Signing them was considered a coup and upgrading these two positions was critical to our future. Tom and David built a strategy and offered each player $8 million over four years. For a short time, it appeared the media were behind us again. Fans were excited. Expectations for the '94 season were high. I believed we would surpass the .500 mark and even win the division.

Then we got the call. Just weeks before training camp, Nate Odomes injured his knee in a basketball game. He had torn a ligament, required an operation and was lost for the season. It was a big blow to the organization, as was Nate's insistence that his orthopedic surgeon perform the operation. Despite our investment, we would have no control over the outcome. That outcome would prove even more troubling when he returned for the '95 season, only to tear the same ligament the second week of practice. This time, he allowed our doctor to operate. He sat out his second consecutive season and came back the third year, but failed to make the team. We finished the '94 season at 6-10, no improvement on the previous year.

We also knew we needed a quarterback. Two previous first round selections, Kelly Stouffer and Dan McGuire, failed to develop and eventually were released. Then in 1993, we believed our search was over. We signed Rick Mirer out of Notre Dame. He was supposed to be in the mold of Joe Montana and, along with Drew Bledsoe, was one of the top picks in that draft. Although we preferred Bledsoe, our scouts placed Rick just behind him on the draft board. We missed Drew by a hair.

Rick had a good rookie season. He showed a strong arm and leadership ability. Rick could also scramble. We believed this was what we needed to make things happen on the field. His challenge was being able (or unable) to read defense. His tendency was to focus on only his first or second receiver, allowing cornerbacks to play off his eyes. His interceptions climbed and his touchdown and passing statistics declined at a steady rate.

Even with a new quarterback, we didn't improve our record. I realized the time had come to make a change at the head coach position. It was a decision that would prove to be as difficult as anything I'd done professionally. Tom was a long-time friend. I had talked him into coming to Seattle. He had the respect of the players and was a proven winner. But it was not working with the Seahawks.

Our conversation wasn't long. He realized a change was necessary—anything to find the chemistry needed to win. We brought in Dennis Erickson, a college coach who had won two national championships at the University of Miami. Despite his appointment, we still did not improve the next season. We still had a problem at quarterback and we were playing in probably the toughest division in the NFL, the AFC West. During the first half of the 1990s, it seemed like the Chiefs, Chargers and Broncos were always in the playoff picture.

Things got worse. Under the new 1993 collective bargaining agreement with players, several teams began offering huge signing bonuses to them. They'd be paid over several years. With this development, I realized we wouldn't be able to compete for players without some big changes. To bring in needed revenue, we'd need a new lease or a new stadium. Among other things, we shared the Kingdome with the Seattle Mariners, and we had to divide our skybox income and advertising with them. We tried to negotiate with the county about our concerns. We wanted money for stadium improvements. The Mariners and Seahawks jointly pursued stadium funding from the state legislature. The legislature declined, and it became obvious that it was going to be almost impossible for us to get a new stadium or improvements to keep us competitive.

I made the difficult decision to either move the team or find a buyer in Seattle who would have a better chance of getting a new stadium. I approached potential buyers in Los Angeles and Anaheim. At the same time, we contacted prospects in Seattle. No one was interested, especially after they investigated our stadium lease.

Finally, I felt I had no other choice. We moved our preseason practice to Anaheim and announced that we would find another home for the team. Seattle erupted in anger. We got hit with many lawsuits to stop us from moving. But the city also got serious about helping us find a buyer. Local leaders finally persuaded Paul Allen, a Seattle resident and the cofounder of Microsoft, to option the team for $200 million. But the state and county had to build him a new stadium.

Allen put down $30 million as a deposit. I'd have to return his money if he failed to get his stadium. He spent millions of dollars on a campaign to persuade voters to approve a new facility. While we had originally requested only $120 million to modernize the Kingdome, the government would now be contributing $300 million to build the new stadium. The referendum barely passed. We closed the sale at the end of 1997.

Once again I was starting over—without football, but with the money and time to look for real purpose in my life.

Chapter 7:
MAMMALS, MUSEUMS AND AUTOMOBILES

No person has been honored for what he has received; always, for what he has given.

Anonymous

I've achieved more financial success than most people dream of. I've made hundreds of millions of dollars and owned a professional football team. I fly around the world in my own private jet. I liked that lifestyle. I still like it. But you get to the point in life where you look at yourself, look at the country you are in and realize it's been extremely good to you and it's time to give something back.

It began with a passion for cars. It was my strongest indication to date that there could be more to life than just the next deal. I realized I could use my money for a larger purpose. Given what was to come in my life, it's appropriate that it started with wheels.

This twist in my road to purpose began with my plans for the Blackhawk Country Club. I wanted to make it prestigious, one of the finest in the United States. My team hired chefs, captains and waiters from Miami's best hotels and designed exclusive rooms for private dining. After it opened in 1980, it was featured on *Lifestyles of the Rich and Famous* as one of the best clubs in the nation. As part of the benefits, I thought a Rolls-Royce limousine would be attractive for use for weddings and important events at the club.

I heard about a Rolls-Royce Silver Wraith for sale by a classic car dealer in Arizona. When I flew to look at it, I bought it. But the transmission needed work. A lot of work. Two months later, when it still wasn't fixed, I went back to the dealer. Like any unsatisfied customer, I asked for my money back. But the salesman assured me it would be fixed. I trusted him. I ended up buying three more cars from him: A 1937 Cord Sportsman, a 1939 Lincoln convertible coupe, and a 1928 Cadillac Dual-Cowl Phaeton convertible. He convinced me they were good buys. For once, I'd met a better salesperson! He ignited my interest in classic cars and I was hooked. He impressed me so much that after I returned home, I thought that I should hire this salesman and start a classic auto collection.

That salesman was Don Williams. He was enthusiastic about the chance to put together a group of the some of the finest classic cars in the world. After I hired him, we heard about an incredible collection of 13 cars for sale in England. The first time we became aware of it, we knew it was the greatest collection on the market at that time. We traveled to Europe and negotiated a multimillion-dollar price for it. The purchase needed to close immediately. Otherwise, a bank was going to take possession of the cars and their price would double. I called a friend at Bank of America and explained the situation. I asked him to wire me the money. We'd take care of the details later. Luckily, he agreed. With that, we owned an impressive collection of some of the world's great classic cars. We were still used car dealers at heart, and classic automobiles are the most desirable used cars.

It was the start of an endless global buying spree in search of the

world's greatest cars. Our stockpile grew with new purchases and
trades. Sometimes we'd even buy a collection of 100 cars just to get
the three or four gems. The history, beautiful craftsmanship and
artistry of these classics thrilled me. But their purchase, storage and
maintenance were expensive. Then it occurred to me: the cars were
just as impressive as pieces of artwork. They deserved to be shared
with the public in a classic auto museum. I started working on plans
to set one up. That way, people from all over the world would be able
to enjoy them.

I approached several universities as possible partners. At the
University of California (UC), Berkeley, I met Michael Heyman, the
chancellor. He was intrigued by the idea of an automotive museum.
Under my proposal, the university would eventually own the museum and many donated cars. That excited him. We agreed to an
arrangement. One part of the museum would house antique cars; the
other part would exhibit some of Berkeley's treasures in anthropolo-
gy and paleontology, an important area of study for children.

Always the developer, I had the museum constructed as part of a
shopping center at Blackhawk. I hoped it would draw people to shop
when they came to see the cars. The museum opened its doors to the
public in September 1988. The building turned out to be strikingly
beautiful and showed off the cars as the masterpieces they are. The
collection was worth $100 million. To help get kids to the museum,
we started the Children's Education & Transportation Fund, which
helps pay field trip expenses for museum visits by public, private
and parochial schools in Contra Costa County. It's the only fund of its
kind in the San Francisco Bay area.

Today, the Blackhawk Museum is recognized around the world. It
currently displays about 100 classic cars, many of which are one of a
kind and date from around the turn of the century. Some of them are
on loan to us from friends who own some of the finest private collections in the world. Some of these cars would never be seen by the

public were it not for the museum. The display evolves and changes constantly. Over the years, the museum has displayed Clark Gable's 1935 Duisenberg roadster, Franklin Roosevelt's 1938 Packard Phaeton, Rita Hayworth's 1953 Cadillac coupe (one of two in the world) and Queen Elizabeth's 1954 Daimler limousine, among many others of note. Blackhawk has the most dramatic presentation of coach-built cars in the world, without exception. This unique collection ensures that significant automotive treasures that blend art, technology, culture and history will be exhibited for public enjoyment as well as educational enrichment for years to come.

Twelve years after we opened the museum, UC Berkeley decided it was too far from campus and withdrew some of its educational support. So with the university out of the picture, we expanded the educational focus of the museum with a number of rotating displays, including one of the world's great collections of automotive art. In 1999, my son David headed the museum for four years and initiated and expanded its role as an affiliate with the Smithsonian Institution. Numerous world-class Smithsonian traveling exhibitions were brought out and displayed to the public during this period. Now we are replacing them with a wheelchair gallery—an educational multimedia exhibit about the history of the wheelchair and the mission of the Wheelchair Foundation, which I founded in 2000 (I discuss it at length in subsequent chapters).

I'd been interested in education for many years, beginning with the teacher awards Pat and I started at my sons' high school in Florida in the 1970s. Our programs at the museum made me more aware of education than ever before. I realized that many children didn't have access to the quality schools and opportunities that my sons had. Though I only completed high school, I know that my success without formal education is unusual and that I grew up in a much different world than the children of today. Children need a good, solid education. The best way to ensure that they get it is to support teachers.

I looked again to UC Berkeley for help on a new education initiative. I had developed a good relationship with the officials there through the automotive museum. Later, I had contributed to the university's Museum of Art, Science and Culture. Through Berkeley, I saw a way to bring more needed support to teachers.

The California public school system faced (and still faces) overwhelming problems. Teachers cannot reform schools in my state without principals who promote change. So I decided to try to reform the schools another way, by establishing the Principal Leadership Institute with Berkeley. I helped launch it with a $7.5 million gift.

The Institute opened in 2000. It prepares educators to be effective leaders in California's urban schools, where reform and improvement is most needed, but also most difficult. The majority of the students accepted into the Institute are teachers from inner-city schools. The funds I donated to the program provide scholarships that cover the cost of the $10,000 tuition of each student. After an intensive 14-month program of night, weekend and summer school courses, students receive a master's degree in education. They also earn a recommendation for their Administrative Services Credential, which is required to become a principal. Graduates agree to serve in a leadership capacity in a California public school for four years.

With this Institute, UC Berkeley developed a progressive program that redefines the roles of principals and creates reform-oriented leaders, committed first and foremost to improving teaching and learning in their schools. The first class of Behring Scholars completed the program in August 2001. Every year at the graduation ceremony, I am moved by the desire, motivation and devotion expressed by the graduates. Knowing I had a role in helping inspire leadership in our state's schools gives me a good feeling.

As a result of my business success and my charitable work, I began receiving national recognition. I am particularly proud of one tribute. On Sunday, June 25, 1989, I was honored along with some of the most recognizable people in America. That night, I found myself with 400 guests and students seated at tables throughout a ballroom in San Francisco. I felt a bit out of place—a bald, bulbous man sitting with Oprah Winfrey, George Lucas, Bob Woodward, Henry Mancini, Dinah Shore, Tom Brokaw, Beverly Sills, Ralph Lauren and the other famous inductees into the American Academy of Achievement.

They must have been wondering, "Who is this man? Why is he here?" More than one mistook me for Alfred Hitchcock, who had died nine years earlier.

The American Academy of Achievement was established in 1961 to, as its mission statement reads, "inspire youth with new dreams of achievement in a world of boundless opportunity, to broaden the recognition of men and women of exceptional accomplishment in America's great fields of endeavor, to champion the spirit of free enterprise and equal opportunity for all, and to foster an international spirit of understanding by annually bringing together the great minds and talents of other nations."

Each year, over a long weekend, the Academy brings together hundreds of America's brightest students with men and women who have distinguished themselves in their respective fields—business, art, science, education, government and sports. It provides the young people two days of one-on-one conversations, conferences and networking with Academy members. At the end, new inductees are recognized at what is solemnly called the Banquet of the Golden Plate. General Douglas MacArthur, Chuck Yeager, Helen Keller, J. Willard Marriott, Ray Kroc, Neil Armstrong, Steven Spielberg, Michael Jordan, Donna Karan, Robert De Niro, Gerald Ford and Bill Gates are just a few who have received the Golden Plate over the years. Each of them is outstanding in his or her field. Each has touched the lives of others and left the world a little better off.

I sat in the ballroom looking at the 40 members of my class.

They included Kareem Abdul-Jabbar, Ernest and Julio Gallo, Vartan Gregorian, William Hanna and Joseph Barbera, Arthur Mitchell, Charles Schwab, Tom Selleck, Bill Walsh, Steve Wynn and John Sununu. As I considered the list of current and former recipients of the Golden Plate, it struck me that while there was diversity in age, careers, accomplishments and interests, there was one quality that each recipient shared: all were leaders who had inspired others to believe in them. They did that, as far as I am able to determine, with vision and credibility. They could imagine what others could not, and they had the ability to inspire others to enlist in their cause.

In addition to the people I have met through the Academy of Achievement and my business career, I've been honored to know other accomplished and celebrated leaders in the world. They have shaped my outlook and helped form much of my charitable work. One of my mentors in philanthropy is King Juan Carlos of Spain, who has become a good friend. He has introduced me to many people. He has given me insight into world problems and what needs to be done to create a more friendly and peaceful world. I've also been privileged to meet and know Nelson Mandela, former French President Valery Giscard d'Estaing, Mikhail Gorbachev and other leaders. They have also greatly influenced me by demonstrating some of the qualities needed for leadership and how to deal with the events that change the world.

About the time I started collecting classic automobiles, I developed another passion—big game hunting. It became part of my charitable activities as well. My financial success allowed me to travel to one of the most exciting places in the world—Africa. I was captivated by its undeveloped beauty and enthralled with the challenge of hunting some of the most powerful creatures on earth. Although I know many people do not approve of hunting, I've always been intrigued by the skill and determination required for the sport. I started hunting as a kid in Wisconsin. Today, I hunt in what I consider to be a responsible manner, respecting all legal quotas and paying required fees. The hunting fees I pay help fund conservation research, operations of schools and hospitals and poaching prevention in tribal lands. I belong to Safari Club International (SCI), an organization that promotes hunting but also funds research and conservation initiatives. SCI's 42,000 members include retired General Norman Schwarzkopf, former President Bush, an honorary lifetime member, and other notable people.

After years hunting in Africa and other parts of the world, I had a large collection of mounted animals. I felt the specimens would be ideal for museum or educational purposes. I contacted several natural history museums to see if they needed any new animal displays. I went first to the American Museum of Natural History in New York. Although it was interested, it didn't need more specimens. By chance, I thought of Mike Heyman from Berkeley, who was now the secretary of the Smithsonian Institution in Washington, D.C. When I called him in 1997 to ask if he knew of a museum that might be interested in my collection, he said, "You have found one. How soon can you be here?"

I flew to Washington. We toured the Smithsonian's collection and looked at the animals, many donated by Teddy Roosevelt. Many specimens had seen better days. Mike explained to me that not only did many of the current specimens need repair, but the science and educational exhibits desperately needed to be updated. Excited by the idea of sharing my enjoyment of amazing animals, I decided to donate $20 million and the best of my collection of mounted animals and animal skins to the Smithsonian. This money helped the Smithsonian build the finest mammal hall in the world. It includes hands-on interactive exhibits and impressive dioramas that explain how mammals have evolved and adapted to habitat changes over millions of years. It took three years to complete the 25,000-square-foot gallery.

The Kenneth E. Behring Family Hall of Mammals displays a wide variety of animals, from rainforest to desert dwellers, from the Australian koala to the American bison. Not only is the scope impressive, but the presentation is unique. One display lets visitors feel how cold it is for an Arctic squirrel as it hibernates in its burrow at a 34 degrees below zero. Displays of African watering holes are enhanced with the sounds of intermittent rainstorms. The hall houses 274 specimens in all, including such greats as a leopard, a lion, a walrus and a brown bear. Teddy Roosevelt's prized white rhinoceros is there, too.

The exhibit opened in the fall of 2003. It took longer to complete than I expected. But I'm proud to have my name associated with it. It has set a standard for the other halls of the Smithsonian, as well as for museums around the world.

I suppose the Smithsonian knew a good thing when it saw one, because it continued to court me. After Mike Heyman resigned, Lawrence Small became the secretary of the Smithsonian in 2000. He asked about my other museum interests. Looking back on my roots in the poverty of the Depression, I knew that I'd come a long way from the boy who owned a single pair of overalls. I also knew that I owed a debt of gratitude to the country that had allowed me to achieve my dreams. I was inspired to show the history, opportunity and future that can be attained with the freedom we have in America. The Smithsonian wanted to revamp the National Museum of American History. It sounded like a fit. I agreed to donate $80 million to modernize the museum's exhibits and to showcase the American Dream in the nation's history. I can think of no better way to repay my country than to pay tribute to the people who made it, and continue to make it, the greatest country in the world. One of the first exhibits to benefit from my donation was "The American Presidency: A Glorious Burden." It opened in 2000.

In November 2004, the Smithsonian opened the next exhibit planned under my gift, "The Price of Freedom." It covers the history of the U.S. military from the colonial era to the present. It presents and explores how wars have shaped America's concept of freedom and defined its role as a world leader. Among the 700 objects in the 18,500-square-foot space are the two chairs and table used by Grant and Lee at Appomatox to sign the surrender documents that ended the Civil War, Colin Powell's woodland camouflage uniform, the nameplate from the battleship Maine, a regimental flag carried by black troops from the Civil War and a Vietnam combat "Huey" helicopter that carried troops into battle and out of harm's way. It also includes a showcase for winners of the Congressional Medal of Honor, the nation's highest military award. The "Price of Freedom" exhibit focuses on contributions Americans have made in critical moments of our history and honors the personal sacrifices of both soldiers and civilians. I hope that citizens will leave it with a better understanding of the price of freedom that we sometimes take for granted in our nation today.

My experiences with the Smithsonian convinced me to contribute to other museums, this time outside of the United States. In 2004, I agreed to help develop three mammal exhibit spaces for natural history museums in China—in Shanghai, Dalian and Yangzhou. We are currently working on the designs and assembling collections so that millions of Chinese children and adults can learn about Africa and other areas that I've had the good fortune to visit. For many Chinese, it will be their only first-hand experience with this astonishing wildlife and its habitats.

As I look back over the contributions to museums and education, I'm proud that my financial success has allowed me to give something back. While my charitable activities began at my sons' high school in Florida many years ago, participating in these organizations laid a new path before me, one much more meaningful than simply making money. But my most life-changing philanthropic experiences came not from these large financial contributions in the United

States. They started in small rural villages in the heart of Africa and would take me on a journey around the world.

Part IV:

Purpose

Chapter 8:
EPIPHANY IN ROMANIA

Life without hope is life without meaning.

Anonymous

There are some experiences that change you forever. They leave you with a different impression of the world and the people in it, and you are forced to act on this new understanding. At least I've been forced to act on it. Robert Berdahl, chancellor of the University of California, Berkeley, once described me as "a man who sees a need and responds immediately." From my earliest days as a used car salesman turned snowplow operator, I've always reacted quickly to any situation involving a need waiting to be filled.

In a remote village in Romania in 1999, a handful of people exposed me to a world that I never knew existed. Their simple wish to enjoy freedom of movement required me to take action. Meeting them and thousands of people in the world with this same desire has altered the path of my life. It has brought me true joy. It has helped me to find real purpose.

This journey began in Africa. In the 1990s, I was making frequent hunting trips to Zambia, Zimbabwe and Namibia. Our hunting parties included local trackers and professional hunters. They'd take me to villages to visit schools and health clinics. Though I'd grown up poor in rural Wisconsin, nothing prepared me for what I saw. The hospitals were sometimes single large rooms partitioned off so that women in labor were barely separated from children with malaria or people waiting for surgery. The beds were small and sometimes not even covered with sheets. The facilities were so overcrowded that sometimes people had to lie on the floor. Doctors and nurses didn't have adequate medical supplies or equipment. I was shocked by the conditions.

Schools also lacked basic necessities. Usually they were nothing more than a simple shelter without doors or windows. In some places, they consisted of a few sheets hung from tree branches. Kids came to class barefoot; there were no books or supplies for them. Teachers had difficulty teaching them reading and writing, let alone anything beyond basic skills, because of the lack of educational materials. So by the second or third grade, many children lost interest in learning. I met devoted teachers who were discouraged because they had difficulty keeping the children in class. They felt that because their students couldn't get a decent education, they would simply return to the same impoverished village life of their parents and would be unable to improve themselves or their communities. Their comments struck me.

When I returned home, I started looking for medical and school supplies to bring back with me on my next trip. Because there are so many different languages and dialects within single countries in Africa, their governments encourage people to learn English. In many places, it's become the unifying language and the language of business. One of the best tools for teaching people English is through children's books, which are written simply. I contacted some school districts in California that were replacing some of their older texts for first-, second- and third-graders. They agreed to donate these old books to African schools. My friends in the Bich family even agreed to donate 100,000 Bic pens. I gathered these and other supplies and packed them into my plane to take to Africa. On my next trip, my team and I made sure the items were distributed in needy villages.

Each time I returned to Africa, I brought a load of medical supplies, school supplies or clothes to the villages near the places I was visiting. Eventually shipments got so big that I arranged for some of them to be shipped in separate containers. I felt the materials were making a difference in the communities that received them.

Charitable organizations in the United States heard about what I was doing and started to call me with requests. In 1999, LDS Charities asked if I could deliver supplies near the route we were taking to Africa. LDS Charities is the humanitarian outreach branch of The Church of Jesus Christ of Latter-day Saints. It provides assistance to people in need, regardless of race or religion worldwide. When families were forced to flee Kosovo in the 1990s, LDS Charities responded immediately with food, clothing, blankets and personal hygiene kits. The organization needed to deliver 15 tons of canned meat quickly to the refugees there and asked for my help. I agreed. When we loaded the plane, we had room left in the hold. Some of the volunteers asked if I wouldn't mind stopping in Romania to deliver wheelchairs to a hospital there. We had the space for six wheelchairs. Little did I know that these six wheelchairs would alter the direction of my life.

After delivering the meat to the refugee camps, I flew to Romania. The hospital wasn't as bad as those I had visited in Africa, but it was not in good shape. In the United States, we take for granted that our hospitals will be clean and sanitary and have all of the medical supplies we might need. That's not the case in much of the world. I met the director in charge of the hospital when we dropped off the wheelchairs. He showed me around the facility and talked to me about the lives of people with disabilities. He said that in poor and developing countries, many people with physical disabilities are basically discarded. They often aren't treated as human beings. As a result of their illnesses or inability to move, they and their families are stigmatized. There's a common belief that if a child is born with a physical disability, it is punishment for something that the families have done wrong. In many parts of the world, the disabled are treated as if they are cursed or possessed by evil spirits. Many don't acknowledge their presence. They are hidden away in the back of a hut and given a single daily meal. Sometimes their families are ashamed to see them crawl or be carried, so they lock them away. I have seen people in boxes in back rooms.

The director introduced me to an elderly man who had lost his wife and then suffered a stroke. He couldn't walk anymore. The man couldn't speak any English, but the hospital staff interpreted his story for me. I told him that I had brought a wheelchair for him so that he would be able to move on his own again. When I helped lift him into the wheelchair, he started to cry. Through his tears, he explained that now he would be free to leave his house when he went home.

"Now I can go outside in my yard and smoke with my neighbors," he said.

All I could say to him was, "I'm happy we could help you." I was deeply moved. I found it unbelievable that this man and others like him were denied the smallest pleasures in life because of their disabilities. I'd never spent any time with immobile people. No one close to me had ever needed a wheelchair. The simple gift of a wheelchair literally transformed this man's life. It meant so much to him.

I have never felt as grateful as I did in that moment. It took so little to give a wheelchair, but yet it meant so much. I was amazed—

I had helped give someone the gift of a new life. I realized that I'd found something tangible and worthwhile, something that sparked an interest within me.

When I returned home from Romania, I thought about what had happened. I had previously seen wheelchairs as a form of confinement. I didn't comprehend the liberation that one could bring to those who are unable to afford them. I was intrigued by the difference these wheelchairs made and I wanted to find other ways to reach out.

I made contact with a charitable organization in Iowa, Hope Haven Ministries, that refurbished wheelchairs and had already planned a delivery to Vietnam in March 2000. It just needed someone to sponsor the shipment. I agreed, as I long as I could join the delivery. In late March, I flew to Vietnam and met the group. We hit our first hurdle in Hanoi. The government would not let the wheelchairs through customs unless it could deliver the wheelchairs itself and take credit for the distribution. We refused.

While we waited to get the wheelchairs out of customs, we went to a hospital. We were told there was a doctor there who could "negotiate" with the government. He agreed to help us but wanted us to tour the hospital first. Once again, the conditions were unimaginable. People were stacked in every room. The facility did not have enough nurses and help to adequately care for patients. The bathrooms and halls were unsanitary. We went into one room that housed three men with leprosy. They were badly disfigured; they had swollen lumps on their hands and feet and growing out of their heads. I hesitated at first, but I felt compelled to talk to them. When I reached out to touch them, they smiled and tears filled their eyes. Someone had finally shown them friendship and affection.

With the doctor's help, we convinced the government to release some of the wheelchairs to us later that day. Party officials would allow 49 wheelchairs to be removed from their headquarters and distributed by our group. The party would hold on to the other 200 wheelchairs.

One of our first deliveries was to a young girl in a small village outside of Hanoi. The trip to her house was not easy. We started out by regular taxi, then switched to bicycle taxi and finally traveled by foot along a dusty path. As we moved through the area, curious people began to follow us. By the time we arrived at the little house, we had close to 50 of them trailing us. We had an interpreter with us; the parents were very nice and gave me tea and a very small chair to sit on. I looked outside and saw an open sewer. I had a hard time drinking the tea.

The little girl, Bui Thi Huyen, was six years old and had never moved by herself. She sat, terrified and crying, on an old pile of rags. I gave her lollipops, but that did not seem to help. We put her in the wheelchair outside her house, where our followers had gathered. I showed her how to put her hands on the wheel rims to move the wheelchair. She was frightened and tearful. But finally, she moved it by herself. Then she broke out into the biggest smile I have ever seen. All of the people clapped and cheered. In a few moments, we had transformed this girl on a pile of rags into a girl who could move about freely. The wheelchair had opened up a new life to her. She could now go to school and build a future. She had found a new world.

We made the long trip back to government headquarters. Once in the building, party workers blared their nationalistic music as we started to distribute the other 48 wheelchairs. It was a spectacle. Physically disabled people came to the distribution on skateboards, in hand carts, crawling on their stomachs, or in the arms of family and friends. We gave the wheelchairs out one by one. Everyone, it seemed, wanted the cardboard boxes the wheelchairs were delivered in. Bystanders clutched the boxes as though the cardboard material were a precious resource.

Many of the wheelchair recipients in Vietnam were victims of land mines, farming accidents, Agent Orange and war. Others had birth defects. They ranged in age from young children to the elderly. They had little in life, but they were resourceful in managing their disabilities. Their stories and dreams moved us.

One woman arrived carrying on her back a boy almost as big as she was. He had cerebral palsy. We were taking pictures of recipients as they received their wheelchairs. When it was time for the boy's picture, the mother said, "Wait a minute." She started grooming her son for the picture. She wiped his face with a rag, combed his hair and arranged his clothes. She wanted him to look as good as possible. It was a lesson in unconditional love. I could see how much she cared for her son, no matter how difficult it was to care for him.

An elderly lady came to me to thank me for her wheelchair. She told me that she was 78 years old. Her teeth were black and broken. She told me that because of her immobility, she had wanted to die but had not been able to. Then she took my hands, came close and smiled and said, "But now I don't want to."

I met a 17-year-old girl who was unable to walk but was the top student in her class. She had a dream of being a doctor. But she was afraid that she wouldn't be able to continue her education because of her inability to get around. To that point in her life, she had to be carried by family or friends wherever she needed to go. I'll never forget her expression of sheer joy and gratitude when she received her wheelchair. Now she would be able to fulfill her dream and attend medical school. The wheelchair helped not only her, but her family and friends, who no longer had to carry her around. Wheelchairs not only improve the lives of recipients—they also change the lives of the people who care for them. We estimate that each wheelchair delivered improved the quality of at least 10 lives—parents, siblings, friends and caregivers.

A young Vietnamese boy had lost the use of his legs early in life.

He propelled himself from place to place on a small plank of wood. His father was a construction worker, and they didn't have enough money to buy a wheelchair. After we placed the boy in the wheelchair, he wasn't sure exactly what to do. But with help from his loving father, he soon figured out how to move around on his new wheels. He discarded the old plank of wood. Once it had been all he had to get around on. But he no longer needed it.

At the end of the distribution, we still had 10 wheelchairs left. We decided to take them to the doctor who had helped us with customs—we figured some of his patients could use them. When we talked to the doctor by phone, he was thankful and said he would have patients ready for us when we arrived. After we arrived, we gave out the wheelchairs and took pictures with the recipients. As we were leaving, someone came to us and said that there was a problem: there were three people in the back of the room who thought they were going to get a wheelchair but did not. These people were crying and inconsolable.

I went to the back. They were the leprosy patients that I had spoken to earlier. They'd heard we were returning to the hospital. Since I had visited them earlier, they were convinced they were going to receive wheelchairs. It was the first time in their lives that they had hoped for something, and now that hope was gone. I talked to them and tried to quiet them; I told them I would attempt to help. We had no more chairs to give, but I would not be the one to dash their hopes.

We drove through the town, desperately searching for more wheelchairs. After several hours, we finally located three used ones. I bought them and brought them back to the hospital. I've never seen anyone as grateful as these forgotten individuals when we placed them in the wheelchairs. They lived in one tiny room together, with nowhere to go and only each other to look at. Leprosy had robbed them of their freedom and dignity. Now they could go outside and sit in the sun, a simple thing that made a world of difference to them.

I returned to the United States filled with a sense of achievement. A month later, the doctor called from the hospital in Vietnam to tell me that the other 200 wheelchairs had finally been released. He assured me that they were given to deserving people.

After Vietnam, Hope Haven asked me to help on other distributions. We did a big one in Guatemala in April 2000. I agreed to pay for the wheelchairs and helped organize the trip there. In Guatemala, the representatives of the first lady, Evelyn de Portillo, met us at the airport and took us to the presidential palace. When we arrived, we were introduced to the first lady and some of the intended recipients of the wheelchairs. She was charming, one of the most beautiful women I have ever met. At the distribution, she took interest in all of the people. She went to each one and held their hands, often kissing him or her. It was a very emotional experience, one that has led to a lasting friendship with her.

After we finished in the palace, we drove to a warehouse in a distant village to distribute more wheelchairs. As I was entering, I saw a man being carried in. He was in great pain and I could see that his leg was swollen. I went to him with an interpreter and asked him what had happened. He said that he had been hurt while working in a field. I asked, "Have you seen a doctor?" He said, "Yes. They had a doctor look at my leg and he said I had gangrene and that I needed to get the leg taken off in the next 30 days or I will die."

The man asked if we could loan him a wheelchair so he could try to borrow the money for surgery. He said, "The doctor wants $100 to cut off my leg and another $25 if he has to put me to sleep during the operation. If I can't get the money, I will have my family bring the wheelchair back to you." I was speechless. Looking at him in his pain, I counted out $125 and handed it to him. He was in shock. He could not believe someone was helping him. The man looked at the money and counted it. Then he handed me back $25 and said he did not have to be asleep for the operation. I gave the money back to him and assured him that I wanted him to be put to sleep. About four days later, he had a nun call to thank me and to let me know that his leg was removed successfully and he was already using the wheelchair. His wife had found a new job and he was going to take care of the house and children. The nun said that the family was happy once again. It's difficult to describe my reaction to this encounter. I was horrified imagining what this man would have gone through had I not been there to help.

We also met an American nurse during the trip. She'd spent most of her life in Guatemala trying to help the poor. She was something else. It's hard for me to imagine completely changing your life that way, giving up everything and focusing only on helping the very poor and unfortunate. To me, constantly doing that kind of work would knock you down, depress you. I loved my experience in Guatemala, but I knew I could return to the life I've always lived. I personally feel the need to effect change on a larger level, to help as many people as I can instead of just a few. This nurse told me she had never been happier than when she was working in Guatemala. She'd found something that gave her complete satisfaction, a purpose in life. I admired her for that.

The nurse led us to another very poor part of the city, to a tiny shack where we met a couple with a little girl. She was about six or seven years old, and she was sitting in a small box. Her mother said she had to work during the day, so she couldn't care for her daughter. The little girl had to stay in the box most of the day. The child didn't know what it was like to move on her own. She couldn't go to school, go outside or even feel the breeze on her face. The woman told me that her daughter wasn't able to go to school because, in Guatemala, unless you are mobile, you have to stay home. It seemed like the most miserable existence I could imagine.

When we gave her a wheelchair, the mother was incredibly grateful. She told us that for the first time, her child would be able to move around the house. It would allow her to go to school and receive an education. No longer would she be condemned to a box. She would have a future.

We completed our distributions in Guatemala and returned to the United States. The people I'd met on my trips had told me tragic stories. They left a lasting impression on me. I realized that there are many people in the world whose lives can be transformed in a simple way. A wheelchair gave them independence and mobility. I had witnessed it firsthand.

But the trips gave me something as well. I've never been an emotional person. But the simple act of giving had allowed me to open my heart. I felt truly needed for the first time in my life, and it was a great feeling. By the time I arrived home from Guatemala, I was certain I'd found the purpose I'd been searching for.

I researched the worldwide need for wheelchairs. It was pretty clear that millions of people in many countries could use them and couldn't afford them. A good basic wheelchair today costs about $500 in the United States; a more advanced one costs hundreds of dollars more. In some countries, that can equal the income for a family for an entire year. No one else was giving away wheelchairs, so why shouldn't I?

It would be a huge undertaking. But I was never one to be discouraged. I decided to create a nonprofit organization to deliver wheelchairs wherever they were needed, without regard to race, religion, politics or nationality. I wanted to reach as many people as possible. My team got to work.

At a press conference on June 13, 2000, we announced the creation of the Wheelchair Foundation. Some good friends joined me. Sen. Bill Frist of Tennessee gave a wonderful speech, as did Sen. Tom Harkin of Iowa. Rep. Ellen Tauscher of California and Rep. Steve Largent of Oklahoma, our former receiver from my Seahawk days, also spoke. Largent gave us one of our first donations. We announced our goal: to distribute one million free wheelchairs in five years. We estimated the cost at more than $150 million. I pledged $15 million to the effort through my personal foundation. Others could contribute $75 to sponsor a wheelchair and we'd deliver it. Our international board of advisors soon included King Juan Carlos, Mikhail Gorbachev and Nelson Mandela. Our new partners included LDS Charities and other charitable organizations. It was the beginning of a mission that would fulfill me in ways that I had never imagined.

I was now passionate about the difference wheelchairs could make in a person's life. The need was enormous. I knew I'd have to raise a lot of money and enlist the support of many others to reach my goals. But I willingly accepted the challenge. Like Theodore Roosevelt's "man in the arena," I felt great devotion and great enthusiasm for a worthy cause.

I had found joy. I had found purpose.

Chapter 9:
OUR JOURNEY AROUND THE WORLD

*A small group of thoughtful people could change the
world. Indeed, it's the only thing that ever has.*

Margaret Mead

In the years since I founded the Wheelchair Foundation, I have
participated in hundreds of wheelchair distributions and have had
thousands of moving experiences. I've met remarkable individuals
who somehow managed to endure in a world that offered them little
hope or meaning. I have watched their lives suddenly become transformed by a simple gift that gave them independence and mobility.

In the two weeks after our press conference in Washington, D.C.,
in 2000, we received requests for 160,000 wheelchairs from non-
governmental organizations (NGOs) that do philanthropic work all
over the world. From the beginning, we have relied heavily on our
partners to meet this demand. Our first partner was The Church of
Jesus Christ of Latter-day Saints. Since we launched the Foundation,
we have worked closely with the church's humanitarian arm, LDS

Charities, to distribute tens of thousands of wheelchairs around the world. "Human suffering anywhere and among any people is a matter of urgent concern for us," LDS President Gordon B. Hinckley has said.

In 2001, we entered into a global relationship with Rotary Clubs, combining funds to deliver wheelchairs throughout the world. This partnership allowed us to deliver a shipping container of 240 wheelchairs (a container is the size of an 18-wheel truck) to just about anywhere in the world for $18,000, or $75 per wheelchair. Previously, we needed approximately $36,000 to make a delivery. (Containers of 280 wheelchairs are now sponsored for $21,000.) We soon adopted this program as our official way of combining resources to reach more people in need.

In the following pages, I write about some of places we have visited, the many people we have met and the joy we have experienced in helping them. We have traveled to so many countries that I have divided the world into regions. Enjoy reading about a few of the people who have changed my life as much as we changed theirs.

Africa

After my business success, I decided I was ready to travel the world. In Africa, I met many people without hope, freedom and dignity because they were physically disabled and did not have the money to deal with their immobility. It was the first place I delivered humanitarian supplies and where I first found purpose.

Zimbabwe

We have made trips to Zimbabwe with the help and company of my good friend Patrick Mavros, a silversmith who lives there. Through his relationship with President Robert Mugabe, we have been supplied with guards for our plane, and one of his army generals assisted us with our deliveries. On one trip in 2001, we arrived by helicopter in the middle of nowhere. All the locals of the village of Mudzi were there to greet us. They had been beating their drums, singing and making homemade beer and food for two days. The tribe's school consisted of a sheet of canvas stretched between two trees; it protected students from the sun. The students had been taught a song in English: "We love you, Mr. Behring." Those were the only lyrics. They repeated them over and over, and I was very moved.

One of the first people we met was a man who had crawled 12 miles on his elbows to come to the distribution. Once in a wheelchair, he started pushing himself around and around. After about an hour of using it, he pulled himself out and sat back on the ground. I asked him through an interpreter, "Why did you get out of the wheelchair?"

"I've had my turn," he said. "Twenty years ago, I had my turn in a wheelchair, too. That is the reason I came back today—so I could have another turn to move myself."

Shocked, I told him, "No, this is your wheelchair."

"I have no money," he said. "It cannot be my wheelchair because I have no money to buy it."

"No, you don't need any money," I said. "We brought this wheel-chair for you. It is a gift." He was overjoyed and thankful.

A year later, we went back to the same area for another distribution. The man was there in his wheelchair; he was surrounded by several small children. "I came back 12 miles," he said, "because I want to show you that the wheelchair is just like new and my children here want to thank you for what you have done for me."

At that distribution, the staff asked me to talk to a young man who had carried a woman for two days and two nights so she could get a wheelchair. I asked him through an interpreter, "Is she your mother?"

He said, "No."

"Is she your relative?"

"No."

"Is she your close friend?"

"No."

"Then why did you carry her for so long to get her here for a wheelchair?"

He said, "She asked me to. Now look at how happy she is. So it was worthwhile." His simple explanation said it all.

But the visit was heartbreaking as well. The locals brought us physically disabled people pulled by oxen in wooden carts. They dumped them in front of us. They were people of all ages, some without legs, other the victims of diseases like polio.

We gave 240 wheelchairs at that distribution. When it was over, the tribal chief invited us to his tent for refreshments and food. The night before, one of our cameramen had sipped some of the tribe's homemade beer. He immediately became very sick and had to be taken to the hospital. So when the chief offered us the same brew, we pretended to drink it. As we left, the people beat their drums, sang and danced. They waved goodbye as we took off in our helicopter, which took us back to my plane. It was the first time they had seen one.

In 2003, my wife, Pat, and a group of Foundation supporters went back to Zimbabwe. The group included Rev. Robert A. Schuller of the Crystal Cathedral Ministries in Garden Grove, California; his wife, Donna; and their three children. The distribution was on the bridge at the famous Victoria Falls, which runs between Zimbabwe and Zambia. When some recipients were unloaded on the Zambia side of the river, they needed help getting to the distribution. The

Schullers and their kids jumped to their rescue, helping recipients with leprosy and other serious diseases.

"All I could think was, 'This is what delivering wheelchairs is all about,'" Pat recalled. "Everyone in the Schuller family and the rest of us were very moved by the experience. These people were some of the neediest we have ever seen. Helping someone into a wheelchair is probably one of the most emotional experiences you can have."

South Africa

We have distributed many wheelchairs in South Africa. One of our partners there is the Englezakis Group, which operates SPAR grocery and convenience stores.

In August 2001, we met in Johannesburg with Nelson Mandela, who is a member of our International Board of Advisors. He had been sick and was going for chemotherapy that afternoon. We spent the morning with him and his wife, Graca Machel, the former first lady of Mozambique. We talked about world events and his life experiences. Because of his illness, we arranged for our distribution to take place at his house. When the wheelchair recipients arrived, Mandela met with each one and gave each child a kiss. I saw for myself what a great man he is and how much he cares for the people of South Africa.

At the press conference after the distribution, Mr. Mandela said, "I am very happy that Mr. Behring has been so generous in bringing us these wheelchairs." Then, looking at me, he said, "It is one thing to ask for help, but when someone comes to you on their own and gives you something without asking for anything in return, this is a sign of true friendship for the people of South Africa."

In July 2003, I had the honor of being one of the guests at Mandela's 85th birthday party, along with former President Bill Clinton; his wife, Sen. Hillary Rodham Clinton; and many celebrities.

That same month, we held a distribution with our friends at

SPAR stores in Pretoria, the capital. One health official there explained, "For many people, a wheelchair would cost a year's salary." A group of about 30 young people came from a center for the mentally challenged near a SPAR store. The group visited the store every Wednesday afternoon; the young people were given special seats in the store where they could sit and enjoy free drinks and cookies. In the past, two children, Theo and Zettie, had not been able to go because they couldn't walk. But on this special day, Theo and Zettie were brought to the store to receive wheelchairs. The other young people clapped and hugged them as they moved around for the first time; they were happy that their two friends had wheelchairs and could now join them on the weekly outings.

At the first township distribution, the people welcomed us with a cheer. They yelled out three times, "Viva Wheelchair Foundation. Viva!" I told the crowd, "We have traveled across the ocean to bring love and hope to the people of South Africa." Several times during the introductory comments, the audience broke out in spontaneous singing. It was beautiful and harmonious. In South Africa, people sing together from the time they are very small; anytime a group is gathered, they sing. As we left, an elderly lady who received a wheelchair said, "God give you more power to help. May God protect you."

After each wheelchair distribution in South Africa, we traveled to Sun City for a celebration dinner to show our appreciation to our partners. We'd also traveled to Cape Town to stay with the Rupert family, one of the most prominent families in the country. The Ruperts have attended wheelchair distributions, and with their help, we hope to continue building awareness about our mission with other local residents.

At one location, attendees included people who had been given wheelchairs at previous distributions. One of the recipients had started to play basketball from his wheelchair; he showed us how he could maneuver. A choir sang gospel songs for us and celebrated with the people who received wheelchairs for the first time.

We met a young lady who told us, "Two years ago, you were here. You were giving wheelchairs away and I was not lucky enough to get one." She added, "Every day and night for two years, I have prayed to God that He would bring you back to bring me a wheelchair. Today, after two years, God sent you back with a wheelchair for me." Then she told us, "And today is my birthday."

In Cape Town, we traveled to a township to observe daily life and to find people in need of wheelchairs. Community leaders greeted us and gave us a tour of a new school they were building and also showed us their brick factory. We were shocked by the living conditions in the village: tin shacks with no electricity, rivers of sewage flowing through the streets and no one working. We asked them if there were any children or adults who needed a wheelchair, because we had one to give away. They told us of a woman who needed help and led us to her home. It happened to be the only cinderblock home in the whole township. We were told to wait outside as the men entered the house and closed the door for a moment.

When the door opened, an old lady emerged, moving with a walker. She was missing a leg. She slowly made her way to us, plopped herself into the wheelchair and smiled. The men told us that she was the oldest person in the community. "She resolves disputes, approves marriages and makes the laws here. The young people should see her in a wheelchair and not in the dirt!" She looked at me and pointed up with her bent fingers. "Now these boys can push me to Sunday school," she said with her gap-toothed smile. "Now when my family comes [meaning everyone in the village] I can counsel them from my new 'red throne.'"

We also visited a center for quadriplegics, where 235 of them lived. The center had one wheelbarrow for its use. Staff members used it only to remove dead patients for burial. We provided 100 wheelchairs to the center, to at least allow them to sit outside in the sun.

Sierra Leone

In Sierra Leone, Anika Olen, a physiotherapist for one of our distribution partners, Mercy Ships New Steps, told us of a man named Abass Conteh. In 1997, he was shot in both legs by rebels. He moved around his village by crawling on his hands and knees. Anika learned that Abass and his older brother were slowly making their way down a dusty road to the distribution. After it began, a messenger arrived to ask Anika if she could change plans. Abass was tired and could not finish his journey, so he asked if she and her team could take the wheelchair to him. She agreed and followed the messenger.

The delivery team and a small crowd went to Abass. When they reached him, he was encouraged to climb into the wheelchair. Abass used his strong arms, which had also been his legs for four years, to roll the wheelchair through the sand for a test drive. The crowd began to applaud. As the team started to leave, several old women came to Anika and held her hands as a sign of their appreciation. They shook their heads and indicated the horror and shame of an adult man who had to "drag his waist" on the ground. They were thankful, as if they had received a precious gift themselves. They prayed for the team. The team appreciated their blessing but felt it had already been blessed by witnessing how a wheelchair could instantly change someone's life.

Botswana

In many African countries, making handmade crafts or clothing is vital to the local economy. During a distribution in Botswana, I met a young woman, about 20 years old. She crawled to us with a piece of leather strapped around her knees and lower body. The leather held in thin, wiry legs—because of poor water quality, she had been born with a birth defect. Her legs had not formed properly. We gave her a wheelchair, but I will never forget her eyes—she had lifeless eyes.

After the distribution, the local people took me to a sewing shop. Across the room, I saw somebody waving at me. It was the young woman. She wheeled the chair to me all by herself and her face beamed with joy. She told me that for the first time, she could learn how to make clothes! She could now make a living! I couldn't believe what I was seeing—the very same day this woman had received a wheelchair, she had received a new life. And there is nothing more rewarding.

Tanzania

In 2002, we scheduled a large wheelchair distribution with the first lady of Tanzania, Anna Mkapa, in Arusha. When the recipients were lifted into their new wheelchairs, one man started raising his arms and shouting in thanks. All of the other recipients quickly joined him. When we asked what they were saying, we were told that they were shouting, "Now we can fly."

In Tanzania, we have also distributed wheelchairs with Raoul and Jan Ramoni, who are friends of mine from safaris. The Ramonis operate and NGO that helps build schools for the Masai people and provides them with humanitarian services. Many Masai are disabled because of mercury in their water. In addition to helping them with wheelchairs, we are working on a project that we hope will give them clean water, so they won't get sick and will have less need for wheelchairs.

Ethiopia

Ethiopia is one of the poorest countries I have ever visited. It's made up of 60 million people in six major ethnic groups. The infant mortality rate is 106 per 1,000 births, compared with 6 per 1,000 in the United States. The literacy rate is 35 percent, compared with 97 percent in the United States. There is only one doctor for every 30,000 people in Ethiopia, compared with one for every 3,000 in the

United States. The average life expectancy in Ethiopia is less than 40 years.

At a distribution in Addis Ababa, the capital, we had given away all of our wheelchairs and were leaving when I saw an elderly woman dragging herself up the street toward us. I went to her to find out who she was and why she was coming late to the event. She was spattered with blood from her shoulders to her wrists. She said, "I heard there was going to be some wheelchairs given away here, so I pulled myself for nine hours in hope that I would get one."

We had given away all of the wheelchairs, but we had some on the plane for our next stop. So I sent some of our staff people to get her one. We washed her arms and lifted her into the wheelchair. I could still see the bloodstains on her arms. One of her legs was bent one way, the other in the opposite direction. Once in the wheelchair, she had a smile on her face; she held my hands as she prayed, and I could see the gratitude in her eyes.

Congo

We were invited to come to the Congo in 2003 to meet the new president, Joseph Kabila, and deliver wheelchairs at his palace. Kabila had replaced his father, who had been assassinated by one of his guards. I was impressed with the new president; he introduced me to four warlords who had thrown the country into civil war for many years. As part of a peace settlement, they had become cabinet members in his new regime. The country desperately needs help—it suffers from 95 percent unemployment.

An eight-year-old boy was to receive a wheelchair; we went to his home first by taxi, then by bicycle taxi and finally on a dirt path by foot. As we continued along pushing the wheelchair, people started to follow us. By the time we reached the boy's hut, we had several hundred people around us. The boy had been told he was getting a wheelchair, so when he saw us, he came crawling to us faster than anyone I had ever seen crawl. He almost jumped into the wheelchair. Once seated, he started wheeling himself around in circles. His brother and sister wanted a ride, but he wouldn't give them one! The crowd around us broke into song; people waved their arms. It became a real celebration.

Angola

Angola is a country torn apart by decades of civil war. It has the largest physically disabled population per capita of any country in the world. We have teamed with ChevronTexaco and Rotarians to get wheelchairs to people there, many of whom are land mine victims. Together, we have given more than 3,000 wheelchairs to the people of Angola, and this is just the start.

In 2003, a Wheelchair Foundation team visited a leper colony in Angola run by Joseph Manual Gush. He informed us that the government of Angola and the World Health Organization were able to provide medication to treat leprosy, but that other aid was in very short supply. The compound the patients lived in was completely fenced and gated. Most of the people suffered from infection on their extremities, and we saw several people who were unable to walk because of infection in their feet. There was a great need for wheelchairs, and we provided more than 20 wheelchairs to the neediest.

A delivery team traveled on another mission to Angola in 2002. It met a group of physically disabled men who were visiting the capital, Luanda, for a wheelchair basketball tournament. They planned to play in borrowed wheelchairs. Each young man had a unique story of how he had lost the use of his legs: one in a farming accident, one in a motorcycle accident, one to a land mine. The team arranged to have wheelchairs delivered to their village so they wouldn't have to crawl to and from school, church and their homes.

"I want to thank you for the wheelchair you are giving me," one of the young men said. "My father ignores me because my disability makes him look bad to other people in my village. The only time that he is proud of me is when I am in a wheelchair playing basketball." The young man paused and could not hold back his emotion. As tears began to form in his eyes, he sat up straight and said to me, "Now my father will be proud of me all of the time, and that makes me very, very happy."

In 2003, ChevronTexaco and Rotary District 5810 from the Dallas, Texas, area joined forces with us to sponsor another 960 wheelchairs to Angola. The joy and the appreciation of the recipients were overwhelming.

Mozambique

In 2001, we traveled to Maputo, Mozambique, for a distribution, with help from the Foundation for Community Development. Some people arrived to receive new wheelchairs by car, some were carried, others came by wheelbarrow and several crawled from their homes, a distance of up to five miles.

Following the welcoming ceremony, everybody went outside to lift the recipients into their new wheelchairs. After several minutes, Saundra Smoak, one of the Wheelchair Foundation volunteers, went back inside the building and noticed a young woman in the back of the room slowly crawling out the back door. Saundra quickly notified the other members of the team. They learned the woman had thought that there were not enough wheelchairs for everyone, so she had begun her five-mile crawl back to her home. They quickly brought her a wheelchair, and her life of crawling was over. Saundra and the team were touched by this woman—driven by hope, she had started her day with crawling five miles, then, misunderstanding, resolved herself once again to immobility. Then, just as quickly, her life changed in a positive way.

"If we give these people hope for mobility, then we must come through for them," I told the group. "If we don't, it's worse than suffering from immobility in the first place."

China

When I first started going to the Far East in the 1960s, I spent time in Taiwan, Hong Kong and South Korea. China was not ready for people like me. But I wanted to go there; I was fascinated by the country and felt I could get close to its culture.

China is an ancient nation with vast land, wonderful people and rich tradition. It is the third biggest country in the world but has the largest population, more than 1.3 billion citizens. As one of the four oldest civilizations, China's written history goes back 4,000 years. In my mind, China is mysterious yet friendly. There is always a lot to explore, from the imperial palaces to cave sculpture, martial arts to calligraphy, noodles to Chinese opera. When you get close and try to understand the culture, you will find a certain connection, which reflects the same humanity that is boundless in this world. China's paradoxes are many: Shanghai's skyscrapers contrast with its old brick houses downtown; Starbucks and McDonald's open their outlets in historic sites in Beijing; rickshaws and taxies compete for tourists in small towns. In all, it is a land where great and fantastic changes are taking place.

My first trip to China was in 1978, to explore business opportunities. At that time, the people dressed only in black, gray or dark blue clothes. The disastrous Cultural Revolution had just come to an end, leaving buildings covered with slogans and posters. The people seemed numb and bewildered. They earned little, and there was little for them to buy in shops. Foreigners were rarely seen in the streets, but wherever they were, they received a lot of attention and hospitable treatment.

In fact, some big changes were taking place that year. As a visitor, I could not see much beyond the society's surface. But what happened next is beyond anyone's imagination. That year, the government started opening China to foreign trade and investment. China began its transition from a centrally planned economy to a more market-oriented one. As a result of those reforms, the country's gross domestic product has quadrupled in the past 25 years. China has become the exciting and dynamic country we see today.

I now fly to China four times a year. I usually land in Shanghai or Beijing, then travel to other cities and towns. Everywhere I go, I see construction sites: old buildings being torn down to make room for new buildings, roads and gardens. There are more and more new cars and buses and migrant workers, making the cities feel even more crowded. There is also a growing middle class, which enjoys such luxuries as the new-model televisions and mobile phones. These new consumers do not have go too far to find the latest fashions from Paris or the latest electronic gadgets from Japan. And in their small home offices, they feel their hearts pound when shares of Sina or Sohu soar or drop on the Nasdaq stock exchange.

Shaped like a rooster stepping into the Pacific, China has a land area of about 9.6 million square kilometers. Its diverse geographic landscape offers a wealth of unique destinations that brings me back time after time. You may have heard of some of them: the Himalayan Mountains in Tibet; the Wo Lun basin in Sichun, home to the panda, and the silk route winding through the western desert.

China is such a big country that its cities and towns are very different from one another in style, customs and living standards. Shanghai is the most dynamic city in China—perhaps in the world. It has an amazing skyline formed by scores of skyscrapers across the east and west banks of the Huangpu River. It is a city full of energy and opportunities. Like New York City, it is a melting pot for people, from expatriates to businesspeople from Hong Kong and Taiwan to local Shanghaiese and laborers from the rural west. Beijing, the capital city, is more political. It's full of officials from the domestic and foreign governments and is the headquarters for many foreign companies that operate in China. There are a lot of historic and scenic spots in Beijing, making it a prime destination for tourists.

I like the small towns like Yangzhou and Taizhou, too, where you can find peace and tranquility. The streets in these towns are clean and tidy, dotted with lovely shade trees. People ride bicycles and rickshaws or walk. Hidden in these communities, however, are some of the most powerful manufacturers in the country.

Each town offers its own beauty. But one thing they have in common is people. I love Chinese people. They are some of the friendliest, smartest, most hardworking people I have ever met. Since we began distributing wheelchairs in China, I have made many friends there. One of the things that impresses me about the Chinese is their hospitality and the way they show their appreciation. Wherever you go in China, the local citizens always share their best with you—their food, their homes, their facilities. They spend time and effort to communicate with you and try to understand your culture. Chinese people are also diligent and talented. More often than not, I meet physically disabled people in China who are good singers, painters or craftspeople. And those who work for the benefit of the physically disabled prove their worth and capability. In all, people are the energy of this country and the driving force behind making China so successful.

Because of its size, China most likely has the largest population of physically disabled people of any country in the world. The China Disabled Persons' Federation (CDPF) estimates that 8.8 million Chinese are physically disabled; other estimates run as high as 35 million. No matter what the number, most immobile Chinese don't have the funds to buy a wheelchair. As a result, we have made a major commitment to distribute wheelchairs in China.

To begin with, we purchase our wheelchairs from four factories there. When we first launched the Wheelchair Foundation, we bought our wheelchairs from operations in the United States and Mexico, then in Taiwan. The wheelchairs from Taiwan were of good quality. But I soon learned that the manufacturers were moving their factories to China because of low labor costs. We shifted our purchases to Chinese factories, which made my feelings for the Chinese people even stronger and gave me a greater appreciation of their capabilities. We have now established a research and development center in Dalian, at Dalian Jiaotong University. We will use new technology to produce better wheelchairs and will introduce sophisticated testing to monitor all of our wheelchairs from any factory for quality and the materials we specify.

We started meeting local politicians and party leaders. In 2001, we established a partnership with the CDPF. It has been a significant and effective partnership, because the work of the CDPF makes delivering wheelchairs to the neediest in China most efficient. In China, almost every immobile person is registered with the organization, which keeps detailed records of their health and status. Through the CDPF, we get a better idea of who needs help. Together, we deliver wheelchairs city by city and town by town.

The CDPF was started by Deng Pufang, the son of China's late president, Deng Xiaoping. He is a well-recognized figure in China, not only because of his special background, but also because of his commitment to the millions of people in China who are physically disabled. In 1968, during the Cultural Revolution, Pufang was pushed off a balcony and broke his back. He has used a wheelchair since that day. He told me that the highs and lows of his life have committed him to humanitarian work in his country. He has established a chapter of the CDPF in every major city in China. For his work, he has received numerous awards, including the Lions Clubs International Award. The Rotarians honored him with a Paul Harris Fellowship. The United Nations has named him one its Messengers of Peace. We asked him to join our International Board of Advisors (he accepted), and he has been a good friend in working for a common purpose.

In 2003, we entered into a partnership with the Chinese Ministry of Civil Affairs to deliver 52,000 wheelchairs to rural areas. In 2004, we teamed with the China Charity Federation to start a program called "Operation Mobility." Its goal is to solicit donations from companies doing business in China, which will be eligible for tax deductions for sponsoring wheelchairs. We hope the program will raise the funds to distribute more than 10,000 wheelchairs a year over the next five years.

Since beginning our distributions in China in 2001, we have distributed more than 51,000 wheelchairs in more than 40 cities and towns. We have entered into agreements with our partners to distribute another 80,000 wheelchairs over the next few years. We were asked to give 500 wheelchairs to the victims of the Tang Shan earthquake that occurred in Hebei province in 1976. It killed hundreds of thousands of people and left tens of thousands immobile. Our distribution day was the 25th anniversary of the earthquake. With local leaders, we gave out the wheelchairs, all of which went to people who had been in bed for 25 years. I shook hands with each of the recipients. Everyone was overcome with emotion.

Each of our donation ceremonies in China is well organized and attended by government officials, volunteers and media representatives. No matter how many recipients there are, I try to shake hands with every one. They are often so happy to receive a wheelchair that they grab my hands tightly and, with tears in their eyes, they smile, because I've told them all I want in return from them is a smile.

In spring 2004, we went to Shenyang to distribute 1,000 wheelchairs. It was a beautiful day. When I arrived at the city square, I couldn't believe my eyes: before me were 1,000 physically disabled people sitting in 1,000 wheelchairs, all of them dressed in red T-shirts and white caps. As a children's band played marching songs, volunteers dressed in the same T-shirts and caps stood in line, waiting to help. Many happy family members and passersby looked on. I gave a short speech, as did a couple of local officials. Then we went down to shake hands with each recipient. That is my routine: I give them a wheelchair, my hand and a smile, along with expressing the love and affection of the people of the United States.

At the distribution, I met Wu Li. Immobile from the age of nine months (she contracted polio), Li could not go to school. But she never gave up. She educated herself and taught herself English from watching television and listening to the radio. When she got her wheelchair, she said, "I can go to a bookstore, market and any place I like. I can study at school or take some training courses."

She went on to say, "I cannot thank Mr. Behring more. He knows what we need most. He has given us mobility. Now we can study, live, work, make friends and contribute to our country."

Then she said, profoundly, "A disabled person plus a wheelchair equals a healthy person." It is an equation that I will never forget.

At a distribution in Chongqing in 2003, I met Jiang Xinglan, a mother from a rural area who lost the use of her legs in a gasoline factory explosion. When I saw her, I told our interpreter that I wanted to talk to her. I walked over as she sat in her new wheelchair. She was crying.

I held her hand and told her, "We are here to not only give you a wheelchair, but also to give you friendship and love." She began to cry harder. She told me that she had seldom left her house in the 10 years since her accident. She has lost one of her legs and the other had been badly injured. Because of her family's low income, she couldn't afford a wheelchair. So she moved herself on wooden blocks. She was raising two children and taking care of her 75-year-old father while her husband worked. "Thank you so much," Mrs. Jiang said. "I have a wheelchair now. I am so happy. I am going to the park with my husband this afternoon, which I dreamed of for 10 years."

Something that simple means so much.

On another trip, I heard the story of a severely physically disabled baby with birth defects who was abandoned in a shopping center in 1993. The police investigated but couldn't find the parents, so they took the baby no one wanted to the Kunshan Orphanage. The staff there named him Kun Sha. By the time he reached the age of two, Sha's condition had improved slightly, but he was still unable to stand on his own. The Amity Foundation in Hong Kong learned of

Sha and funded operations on his fingers, ankles, elbows and knees in 1995 and again in 1997. The orphanage developed a special training program to help Sha recover from his many surgeries.

Two years passed as Sha continued to stretch muscles and ligaments in his determination to walk. With the aid of crutches, he was finally able to do it in 1999. In 2000, Sha began school, where the same spirit and desire to succeed that marked his physical progress drove him to earn good grades and live as normal a life as possible. In 2002, a team from the Wheelchair Foundation made Sha's life even better by presenting him with a wheelchair. I was particularly impressed with Sha, who sang a song at the distribution ceremony titled "Little Boy Seeking Dad." It went:

> *Not afraid of raining, not afraid of snowing.*
> *I only want to find him, even if it's cold and windy and snowy.*
> *I want to see him every day, my Dad;*
> *I'm going to find my Daddy,*
> *no matter what outside looks like.*
> *I'm going to find my Daddy,*
> *To find my Daddy, no matter where he is.*
> *I can't find my dearest Daddy;*
> *If you find him, please ask him to come back home.*

He sang in a glorious voice. The song drove home the point of what it feels like not only to be disabled, but to be abandoned. As he sat next to me, he looked into my eyes and asked me, "Are you my grandfather?" I would have loved to have been able to say "yes." I was very pleased that we were able to give Sha a new wheelchair and help make his life easier and more enjoyable. I also gave the orphanage $1,000 for his education. Later, back home, I told Sha's story to a group of children at a school in suburban Washington, D.C. They had raised money to sponsor six wheelchairs, their pennies, nickels, dimes and quarters dropped into plastic jars in the school library and cafeteria. The kids liked hearing Sha's story.

Other wheelchair recipients have amazed me. We gave Xie Yanhong from Dalian a wheelchair in 2003. He was born without the use of his legs. He used his wheelchair to accelerate an ambitious exercise program. He swam great distances every day to strengthen his upper body. When I returned to China in 2004, he told me he had used his wheelchair to travel to England, where he became the first physically disabled person ever to swim the English Channel! He swam 21 miles from England to France in 16 hours and 44 minutes.

He later wrote me the following letter:

> *Dear Respectable Mr. Behring,*
>
> *This is the second time I meet you. Last year, when we first met from the wheelchair donation ceremony, I didn't realize what a gift you've brought to me until today. I know it is not only a wheelchair, but also you've brought a blessing, a good luck to me!*
>
> *Sitting on the wheelchair you gave to me, I went to the English Channel and successfully swam across over this channel. The challenge is huge. But with the great encouragement from you dear Mr. Behring and with tremendous help and support from my disabled friends, from Dalian CDPF and Dalian government leaders Mr. Xia, I became the first disabled person to meet this challenge and I won! It's your love brought to me the success. If I could, I dream some day I can go to U.S. and challenge to swim across the channel in U.S. again. I want to tell the world I am able!*
>
> *Thank you for your love! I will cherish your love and keep it in my heart for always!*
>
> *Xie Yanhong*

This is what wheelchairs and a simple act of giving can do for people.

At another distribution, I met a 49-year-old man named Shen Linhu, from Wujaing city in Jaingsu Province. Linhu had contracted polio when he was four years old. He crawled from place to place on his knees. He protected them from cuts and scrapes with pieces of old rubber tires, which he tied to his legs. He crawled for 45 years. When we gave him a wheelchair, he wept. Then he smiled. "I have finally grown up!" he said. "I will not need any more tires!"

At another delivery, Lin Yu Liang was a recipient. Mr. Lin also suffered from polio. As a child, his parents carried him to school. They gave him a small wooden stool that he rocked from side to side to move himself, but he mainly stayed at home and dreamed of a normal life. We gave Mr. Lin a wheelchair and later learned that he went back to his village and opened a small "milk bar." Not only that, he got married! He was proud of the fact that he was the only physically disabled businessman in his village. He kept his stool but bragged, "I forgot how to use it."

At a distribution in Shanghai, I met a young man who was paralyzed from the neck down. But he was a fabulous painter—he painted with a brush in his mouth. In gratitude for receiving a wheelchair, he painted a beautiful picture of a peacock for me. I think it is the most incredible thing I have ever seen. I was amazed at his ability to paint so many colors in such a small area. This treasure is now on display in our Wheelchair Foundation gallery at the Blackhawk Museum in Danville, California.

Another wheelchair recipient in Shanghai was Xu Guolaing, who also contracted polio as a child. His mother had to take care of him. He attended school occasionally, but most of the time he stayed at home and moved around his house on wooden stools. When he grew up, he suffered from severe vertebra disease. When he received a wheelchair from us, he said, "I can go out to anyplace at anytime to my heart's content. I won't repeat the way of living before. The days of staying at home with my parents are history!"

In Shanghai, I also met Chai Goudong, a middle-aged man who was injured in an accident in his youth. He had a pretty daughter studying in middle school. He had used crutches for years and at times felt ashamed—he said his disability prevented him from "carrying out a father's duties." He said his daughter had to take care of him sometimes. But when he got his wheelchair, he smiled and told me that from then on he could walk with his daughter and do many other things.

Not even the severe acute respiratory syndrome (SARS) scare could keep me away from these wonderful people. SARS is a serious respiratory illness that researchers believe originated in the Far East after 2000; it killed hundreds of people there. But while the West was shunning China, I traveled there. Physically disabled people were depending on me and I was not going to let them down. My trip was written up in national newspapers. Such volunteerism is a concept foreign to many Chinese, and they try to understand the motivation. I tell them it's simple: I get more in return from being here with you than you get from being here with me. And I tell them that the wheelchairs are not just a gift from me, but from many wonderful people in the United States.

They are beginning to understand.

We have delivered wheelchairs to the remotest parts of China, including Tibet. In Tibet, the average healthy farmer can make a few hundred dollars a year, but the disabled struggle. In late 2000, thanks in part to a grant from the Christopher Reeve Paralysis Foundation, we were able to provide 240 wheelchairs to the Tibetans of Kham and other needy and deserving people in Sichuan Province. We worked in partnership with Wheels for Humanity and the Kham Aid Foundation. A Kham Aid field team coordinated efforts on the ground with two local humanitarian groups to identify people in need and bring back their stories.

They told us about Jing Xiaoyong, a 25-year-old man who was physically and mentally disabled from a fever he suffered as an infant. Cared for by his mother, who was unable to move him, Xiaoyong spent most of his life in bed inside a small wood dwelling. Kham Aid President Pamela Logan recalled that Xiaoyong's face was "the palest I've ever seen on a Tibetan." A wheelchair brought the sun's warmth to that face, and a smile was not far behind. Logan explained, "Xiaoyong looked wondrous, as if he had suddenly been beamed to a never-dreamt-of world. When David [a Wheels for Humanity team member] tilted the chair backward to go over the doorsill, Xiaoyong broke out in a huge grin. He loved it! After 25 years in bed, a tilted chair was like a roller coaster."

Like Xiaoyong, many recipients were grateful but shy. However, one 70-year-old Tibetan man named Zhang Dongwen would not accept a wheelchair until he had made a speech through an interpreter. The spontaneous orator addressed the group, saying, "You have come so far to this remote place to help us. On behalf of disabled people here, I thank you. For disabled people, self-sufficiency is really important. We want to take part in the opening and development of this area. I promise to do my best to take advantage of this gift."

Zhang Dongwen's words cut to the heart of what the Wheelchair Foundation's mission is all about. For some, a wheelchair is a means of leaving the prison of a small room. For Zhang and many others, a wheelchair is also a tool for independence and participation in the betterment of a community. Because Zhang and others like him are now able to work in Kham, their neighbors would now see the contribution people with physical disabilities can bring to them.

In January 2004, I participated in wheelchair distributions in several Chinese provinces. In one particularly touching moment, Zhou Li, a representative of the Harbin Daowai District Disabled

Persons Association, read the following message after receiving her new wheelchair:

Dear Friends and Guests,

I am so honored and excited to be here. On behalf of all the people who have received a wheelchair from the Wheelchair Foundation, we offer our sincere thanks to Mr. Behring, his Foundation team and to all the friends who have offered your warm hands to us—Thank you!

We are a special group of people in society. Disasters and diseases have deprived us of walking. We cannot walk nor live as normal people do. Our physical disabilities bring us unimaginable difficulties in daily life, as well as great mental pain. But deep in our hearts, we are longing to live life as healthy and sound human beings! We dream that some day, we can walk, we can move ourselves to go outdoors, to have a look at the beauty of nature; at our beautiful city; to witness the magnificent progress our country is making; and to say hello to the fast-changing world.... Today our dreams are coming true! Thank you so much for bringing us the ability to realize our dreams, to achieve our mobility with the help of a wheelchair. This is such a wonderful experience for us, especially for those who have never walked or moved by themselves since the day they were born! We feel the warmth and strength offered by a pair of warm hands from across the ocean, we feel the love and friendship coming from a worldwide family. We are so thankful and full of confidence! As disabled people, we can only hope to grow stronger, to break through the difficulties of life, and try to greet every day with a smiling face!

Thank you Mr. Behring and the Wheelchair Foundation. You are messengers of worldwide love and friendship!

At that same distribution, I met a smiling 13-year-old girl named Chengxin. She contracted polio early in life and had no use of her legs. After we gave her a wheelchair, she excitedly told us, "My father used to carry me to school every day on his back. As I grew heavier, I worried about him. Now I don't need to worry. I can even go out to enjoy a long walk with my parents."

"The greatest thing is that I can now move anytime I want," she said. "And I don't need to stay in the classroom all day long. With the help of my friends, I can now go outside to enjoy my break time like they do."

"I will never forget Mr. Behring. He is just like my grandfather," she said, crying. "And I have a dream. I want to study very hard, and when I grow up, I want to do the same kind of things for other disabled people as Mr. Behring has done for me. This wheelchair is not only a chair, it is a beam of sunshine that warms my heart, and I want to share the sunshine with many people."

Her final words were, "All children like me can help themselves by believing in our abilities, not our disabilities!" Those words meant more to me than I can tell you.

Our work has been welcomed in China. At a dinner in 2001, the mayor of Shanghai told me, "We did not ask you to come here. You came here because you wanted to help our people. You came here with no strings attached. That is true friendship."

But the needs of the physically disabled will only grow in China as its population ages. One expert at Peking University in Beijing told me that by 2050, China will have more than 80 million people over the age of 80, and many will be immobile.

Our philanthropic work in China is increasing beyond wheelchairs. I am providing mammals for exhibit and educational programs to the Dalian Natural History Museum, the Shanghai Science and Technology Museum and the Yangzhou Slender West Lake Animal Museum. I am working with four Chinese universities researching technology for producing pure water at low cost to the entire world. We hope we can be ambassadors between the China and the United States to share knowledge, friendship and understanding.

Asia

I have enjoyed the many countries and cultures of Asia in the last 20 years. In Thailand, I delivered wheelchairs with King Bhumibol Adulyadej and his daughter, Princess Maha Chakri Sirindhorn. In South Korea, I have been helped by Kun-Hee Lee, the chairman of Samsung, the giant electronics company. He has been very generous to the Blackhawk Museum and the Wheelchair Foundation. Chung Mong-Koo, chairman and CEO of Hyundai Motor Company and Kia Motors Corporation, has been generous as well; he surprised me with a check for more than $150,000 for the Wheelchair Foundation when I visited him at his company. I'll also never forget a trip to Mongolia: I flew in a large Russian-made helicopter to a remote area, and on the way back, it ran out of fuel and crash-landed about a mile short of the airport! We were okay, but I could do fine without any future experiences like that one!

Of course, some of my most memorable memories of Asia come from our wheelchair distributions there. We have been fortunate to work with many wonderful organizations in the region, including the Hanoi Women's Union in Vietnam, the Red Cross in Cambodia, the Foundation for the Welfare of the Crippled in Thailand and the National Rehabilitation Center in Laos.

Philippines

A Wheelchair Foundation team went to the Philippines in 2003 and was introduced to a father and daughter. He told us that she was eight years old and had never been able to go to school because she didn't have a wheelchair. Now that we were giving her a wheelchair, she would start school immediately.

At first, she wasn't able to make the new wheelchair move and was quite distracted by all the attention she was getting as the team took pictures and talked about her. As things began to wind down and conversations turned away from her, she began to pay more attention to it. The team watched her from the other side of the room as she slowly, cautiously placed one hand and then the other on the wheels. Her face was determined as she managed to make herself move about a foot. She did this for about 10 minutes, slowly inching her way across the floor, being careful not to be noticed.

Before long, everyone realized that she had pushed herself to the opposite side of the room. The little girl stopped and acted as if nothing happened, then she looked at the group with a big smile. Later, her father said, "I have carried her since birth. She has never seen a wheelchair until today. She is a smart girl, and that is why this wheelchair is so important, so she can go to school!"

In Manila, our LDS Charities partners met a 13-year-old girl named April. Because of her immobility, she also had been unable to attend school. Her mother had abandoned her family of nine; her father and siblings took care of her. After she received a wheelchair, she enrolled in first grade—seven years late.

"It was wonderful to see her explore the movement of the wheelchair under her own power," said Renn Patch, an LDS representative. "She got ahold of the wheels and made it move. She was ecstatic!"

Vietnam

Vietnam is a poor country. Many people there are physically disabled because of malnutrition and birth defects; others have lost limbs to land mines and unexploded ordnance left over from military conflicts.

At a distribution in Hanoi in 2003, our team met a little boy who moved himself using wooden blocks. He pulled himself along the street dragging his legs. His father brought him to our event and stood silently with the boy in the back of the room. Each time someone received a wheelchair, the boy raised himself up to watch recipients learning to use their new chairs.

When his turn finally came, the boy dragged himself to team members and carefully put his blocks on the ground. Then he lifted himself into the wheelchair under his own power. He reached down to work the brake without instruction. He looked up and, with no change in expression, placed his hands on the wheels and began to move himself around the room. He was very serious about the whole process, but our team knew he had been watching other recipients from the back of the room. He wheeled himself to his father and immediately started smiling and expressing excitement about his wheelchair. The father and the boy whispered to each other. A member of our team asked them, "Is everything okay?"

The father responded, "I am proud of my son because he has passed the test to get a wheelchair." Earlier, the boy had watched so intently because he thought that if he didn't use it correctly, he wouldn't get one. Our team asked the father what he was going to do with the wooden blocks his son used to move. He said, "Tonight my son and I will build a fire at our house and we will burn them together."

Our partners at LDS Charities went to Vietnam in 2003, as part of an 18-day, five-nation mission. They met 18-year-old Vulng Sihung, who had been physically disabled since birth. He received his first taste of mobility with a new wheelchair.

"Before the wheelchair, I would sit alone in one place," he said. "I couldn't do anything. I stayed at home all day in a wooden chair in a very small house. There was no one to help me to go to school, so I never went. Now, with the wheelchair, I will be able to go school and to go outside."

He might cross paths with another recipient, 20-year-old Noc Tu, also immobile since birth. After receiving her wheelchair, she told the distribution team that she was going to go to school. Her father said, "She could not move on her own. All she could do was sit by herself, until she was 10 years old. By the age of 12, she could stand, but she was still unable to walk."

He continued: "I'm very happy and touched that my child received a wheelchair. On behalf of the wheelchair recipients, I'd like to thank the LDS Church and the Wheelchair Foundation.... I don't know what to say but thank you."

A third recipient was a 39-year-old construction worker. While chopping coconuts from a tree one day, the man fell and injured his spinal cord. He was left paralyzed from the waist down. His wife worked while he stayed at home, trying to take care of his 12-year-old son and 5-year-old daughter. He moved around the house very slowly and with great effort.

After receiving a wheelchair, he said, "I am very happy to have this wheelchair. My wife goes to work every day. Now with the wheelchair, I will be able to look after the house and my children. Thank you very much."

In 2003, my son David also went to Vietnam with members of his Princeton class of 1977. After a distribution in Hanoi, one recipient wrote to David:

Dear Mr. David,

Thank you for your undreamed of gift of a wheelchair. I feel very happy. I have learned English for only 3 years now, so please don't laugh. Now I can say that I am the happiest girl because I have a happy family, good friends and especially you, a new friend. My mother said "This is the first time I have met a handsome kind foreigner!" I laughed. I was cold when we met and you gave me my new wheelchair, then you shook my hand and I felt very warm in my heart. I was moved to tears. If only I could see you right now, I could invite you for Vietnamese tea, introduce my father, my older brother, older sisters, and take you to my school with my new wheelchair. Thanks to you I can go to school easier, visit everyone and do everything I like. Thank you very much for your gift from the heart.

Tran Thi Nghua
P.S. Could you send me your photograph?

India

With more than a billion people, India is home to the world's second largest population; it also has a large population of people who need wheelchairs. The prime minister told me that there are about 114 million people in India who are immobile.

One of our Wheelchair Foundation team members, Joel Hodge, tells the story of a family he met on a distribution in Bombay in 2002. The living conditions were horrible, the streets lined with sewage and trash. The family lived in a tin shack with dirt floors. A curtain covered an area in the back of the shack. Joel heard a lot of movement behind the curtain; he was stunned when the mother and one of her sons brought out her other son, who was held to a piece of plywood by wire. He had mild case of a neurological disease. The wires were tied loosely around his wrists and ankles. Joel was shocked. He left the shack to get a wheelchair from the van outside.

Joel and his team placed the 24-year-old son in the wheelchair. He was excited and very animated. Because of his extreme motions, Joel thought the wheelchair would do him no good. But then the young man calmed down and smiled. Joel asked family members why they kept him strapped to a board. The parents replied that he was unable to sit up unassisted but wanted to follow them whenever the family left the house. He would usually fall out of bed trying to get up; when they returned, they often found him face down in the dirt.

After Joel showed the young man how to use the wheelchair, he looked up and smiled; he understood. His sister said he was happy and that she hadn't seen him like this before. Joel wheeled him outside. The young man sat in his wheelchair, looking at everything and smiling. Joel asked his sister if he was able to sit outside very often and she said, "Never, at least not since I was a very little girl. He's always been 'my brother in the back room.'"

Not anymore.

Nepal

In the capital, Kathamandu, in 2001, our delivery team put a young boy into a wheelchair. The boy couldn't speak and hadn't figured out how to move it on his own. Rather, he kept motioning a team member to take him to a nearby water fountain. It took a while to figure out what the boy wanted. But then it dawned on the team member that the boy wanted to play in the water. He also wanted to touch the ivy growing on the walls behind the courtyard of the team's hotel. As long as the team member kept moving him from place to place, he seemed happy. These were things he had never been able to do crawling or lying on the ground. His wheelchair opened up a whole new world for him.

Another man in at the distribution was built like a circus strongman, but his legs were completely paralyzed. He came to the event crawling on his elbows. When the team put him into a wheelchair, he said, "Now I am a man. I have never been a man before in my life. All of my life I have been on my stomach, trying to look up at people. You are not a man when you are on your stomach trying to look up. Now I'm in this wheelchair, and now I am a man. This makes me feel very happy."

Afghanistan

Afghanistan has suffered from armed conflict and oppressive rule for decades. Land mines and unexploded ordnance left over from previous conflicts kill and maim hundreds, perhaps thousands, of Afghans each year. Diseases and accidents also are responsible for numerous disabilities. An estimated 700,000 to 800,000 citizens of Afghanistan are physically disabled.

A team sponsored by Rotarians traveled to Kabul in June 2003 to deliver 240 wheelchairs. One of the recipients was a 19-year-old boy named Najib. He had been confined to his bed for the past 18 months because of an accident. The day after he received his wheelchair, one of our volunteers looked out of his office window: "We noticed a large crowd outside. Najib was the center of attention; he was the hero. He was proudly briefing children on the operation of his new wheelchair. He was surrounded by dozens of curious children asking him how he felt and touching his wheelchair. He said, 'I do not want to go home. I want to go to the shop down the street, and school, and play outside, to feel the outside air.'"

Another Afghan recipient was a young girl who had lost her legs two months earlier when she stepped on a land mine while herding her family's goats. When her father heard about the wheelchair distribution, he carried her on his back to the event. Her family was worried about her; her wounds were not fully healed. Whenever someone moved her, she cried out in pain. Her father said that in a wheelchair, she would feel less pain because no one would have to touch her to move her, allowing her wounds to heal more quickly. The girl and her father were happy to receive a wheelchair. She planned to go to school and learn to live without her legs. Her father thanked the distribution team and blessed Americans who came to the aid of Afghans in need.

I went to Kabul in September 2003 to distribute the first of 5,000 wheelchairs delivered in partnership with the U.S. Department of State, the Department of Defense and with our friends at LDS Charities and the Knights of Columbus. Since 2002, the State Department has provided funds to help sponsor wheelchairs, and the Defense Department has provided transportation of wheelchair containers to countries with land mines and civil unrest. We were met at our plane by five U.S. armored vehicles with machine guns on their roofs. The sight made us all very aware that we were in a war zone. The soldiers escorted us to an armed compound outside Kabul that was to be our home while we were in the country. U.S. military officers advised us that for security reasons, we could distribute wheelchairs only in the compound.

On the day of the distribution, the first buses began to arrive at 9:30 a.m. Officials from the State Department and the U.S. Agency for International Development had measured most of the recipients for their new wheelchairs a few days earlier, so they already had some idea of what was coming.

Family members and U.S. soldiers assisted the recipients as they made their way off the buses. Many were carried, some crawled and some used simple handmade crutches. Everyone took a seat under an awning and each recipient patiently waited his or her turn to receive a brand new, shiny red wheelchair. One of the first recipients was a young man who excitedly wanted to show his new wheelchair agility to the other recipients; he spun around in his new wheelchair, pushed himself in circles and "popped wheelies." Another young man crawled over to his wheelchair but was unable to get into it by himself—the lower half of his body was missing as a result of a land mine explosion. A group of soldiers rushed to his side and lifted him into his wheelchair.

As soon as everyone was seated, we photographed each recipient. With few exceptions, everyone seemed much older than his or her actual age. It's no surprise—the average life expectancy in Afghanistan is only 47 years, and life is often difficult.

As the distribution came to a close, we noticed a man dragging himself along the ground with his hands. A land mine had blown away his entire lower body. His only protection from the rocks and dirt was a piece of cardboard he had tied around the bottom of his torso. He told us he had missed the bus, but hoped there was an extra wheelchair for him. He had a wife and six children; he wanted the wheelchair so he could go back to work and provide for his family. Several soldiers quickly brought him one, and as they picked him up and put him in it, he placed his right hand over his heart and smiled. This was his way of thanking us not only for his new wheelchair, but also for his new way of life.

Throughout the event, I saw many American soldiers moved to tears. They thanked us and the representatives from LDS Charities and the Knights of Columbus for our generosity and compassion for immobile Afghans. The soldiers were grateful for the opportunity to participate in an event that made such a difference to people and spread the joy of unselfish giving.

Cambodia

At a distribution with LDS Charities in 2003, one volunteer met four young men, ages 13 to 19, who were in desperate need of wheelchairs because of birth defects. Some of them didn't have arms, some didn't have legs and some had small stumps with feet on the end. At a Red Cross warehouse, the young men each received a wheelchair. The volunteers emphasized to them that the wheelchairs were to help improve their lives—they were not to be sold. The young men and their mothers were shocked at the suggestion that they might sell them. They thanked the volunteers over and over again for the wheelchairs.

Europe and Eastern Europe

I have enjoyed visiting Eastern Europe; my ancestors came from there. I had the pleasure of holding wheelchair distributions there with Gen. Joe Ralston (USAF-Ret.) in 2001 and 2002, when he was the commander of the North Atlantic Treaty Organization. One of his responsibilities was humanitarian assistance in the region. On wheelchair deliveries, we met with the leaders of Latvia, Estonia, Romania, the Czech Republic, Bosnia/Herzegovina and Hungary. I learned about the new friendships we were forming with these former Soviet satellite countries. Gen. Ralston is now a member of our Board of International Advisors.

As my first wheelchair delivery was in Eastern Europe (Romania), I have returned there many times to help the physically disabled. Here are some of their stories.

Bosnia/Herzegovina

While we were in the former Yugoslavia, we met a Bosnian man who began to cry when he told us of his teenage son, who was very large. While they were walking down a road, the son stepped on a cluster bomb. It blew him up into the air, and he landed on another cluster bomb, which also blew up. Then he landed on a third bomb.

"By the time I got to him, he was covered with blood," the man said. "I was sure my son was dead." The man got his son to a first-aid station. The staff there said the station did not have any blood to help him. Drivers took him to a hospital that had a supply of blood. The man said that as they were going to the hospital, he could feel the life draining out of his son. "But we got to the hospital and God was with us," the man said. His son was treated and lived. He was released from the hospital 11 months later. He had lost both legs at his hips and one arm. He had lost his sight in one eye. He had lost his hearing in one ear. But he was alive.

The father said the only thing his son wanted was to sit in the sun, but he was too heavy for him to carry. A wheelchair would let him do that. We gave his son one. That day, I realized how much a simple thing like sitting in the sun could mean to a human being. Every person should at least have the right to do that.

While distributing wheelchairs in Bosnia, we saw bullet holes in all of the buildings. Land mines left over from the war were injuring 100 people a week. Many people looked very sad. It seemed as though the land mines and chronic unemployment had drained them

The elderly man in Romania who had suffered a stroke and whose plight moved me to start the Wheelchair Foundation (see story page 100).

The elderly Vietnamese woman who told me she had wanted to die—until she got a new wheelchair (see story page 103).

The Guatemalan man with gangrene who did not want $25 from me for anesthesia for his leg amputation. We insisted he take it (see story page 105).

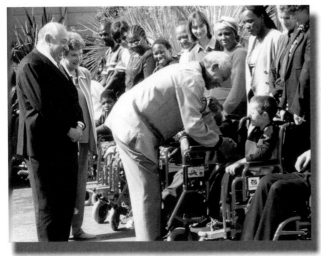

Pat and I in South Africa in 2001 distributing wheelchairs with Nelson Mandela (see story page 114).

The president of Namibia, Sam Nujoma, reads his remarks at our distribution there in 2001.

Dr. Robert A. Schuller from Crystal Cathedral Ministries with his wife, Donna, at our distribution on the bridge at Victoria Falls in Africa in 2003 (see story page 113).

Meeting the first lady of Tanzania, Anna Mkapa, who is a member of our International Board of Advisors (see story page 118).

One of our distributions in South Africa with our friends from SPAR stores (see story page 114).

Meeting with the first lady of Nigeria, Stella Obasanjo, at a distribution in her country in 2001.

In Sun City, South Africa, distributing wheelchairs with our friends from SPAR stores (see story page 115).

Pat and I met a man who crawled to get to our wheelchair distribution in Zimbabwe (see story page 112).

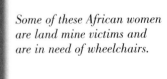

Some of these African women are land mine victims and are in need of wheelchairs.

A man coming to our distribution in Afghanistan in 2003. Most people in his condition are land mine victims (see story page 147).

Wheelchairs can change lives immediately. One minute, this boy in Laos who lost his leg to a land mine is standing with crutches; the next minute, he is mobile in a new wheelchair.

With my good friend King Juan Carlos of Spain (left), and his wife, Queen Sofia, and the president and first lady of Brazil in 2000. The king and queen chair our International Board of Advisors (see story page 173).

Joining Rotarians at their international meeting in Barcelona, Spain, in 2002. Rick King, the organization's president, is in the center front. Dr. Jon Grant is in the back on the right.

*I traveled to Saudi Arabia in 2004 to work on an agreement to distribute
wheelchairs in this vital region of the world (see story page 160).*

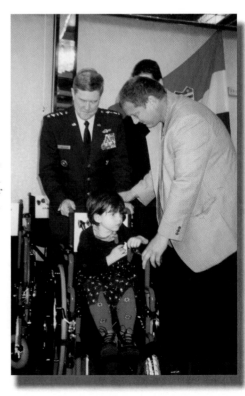

*General Joe Ralston (USAF-Ret.)
helps at a wheelchair distribution in
Eastern Europe. He is a member of
our International Board of Advisors
(see story page 149).*

Meeting with First Lady Ruby Moscoso de Young and her sister, President Mireya Elisa Moscoso Rodriguez, at a distribution in Panama in 2001 (see story page 175).

Distributing wheelchairs in Guatemala with Evelyn de Portillo, when she was first lady of that country (see story page 105).

Pat and I with our friend, Frank Devlyn, the former president of the Rotarians who first got them involved with the Wheelchair Foundation. With us are his wife, Gloria Rita, and the first lady of Mexico, Martha Sahagun Fox (center), who is a member of our International Board of Advisors.

A nun we helped in Nicaragua in 2001 (see story page 168).

Distributing wheelchairs with friends from the LDS Church.

With Angel, the boy in Mexico who said he would "see me in heaven" (see story page 179).

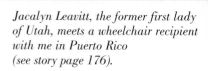

Jacalyn Leavitt, the former first lady of Utah, meets a wheelchair recipient with me in Puerto Rico (see story page 176).

I greet a wheelchair recipient at a distribution in Guatemala

Students at Samuel Tucker Elementary School in Alexandria, Virginia, give
me jugs of spare change in 2004 to use to sponsor wheelchairs (see story page 130).

With Dr. Robert A. Schuller of Crystal Cathedral
Ministries, on the Hour of Power program.

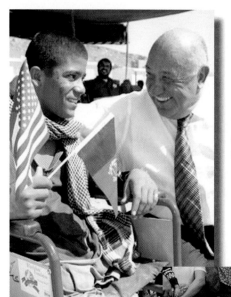

With a wheelchair recipient at our distribution in Afghanistan in 2003 (see story page 145).

With Bui Thi Huyen, the Vietnamese girl I met in 2000, whose joy at receiving a wheelchair helped convince me to start the Wheelchair Foundation (see story page 102).

His All Holiness Ecumenical Patriarch Bartholomew in 2004 at a distribution with me in Turkey (see story page 152).

Receiving a blessing from His Holiness Pope John Paul II in 2004, with my Wheelchair Foundation colleague Charli Butterfield.

A Chinese man helps a family member into one of our wheelchairs at a distribution in China.

Deng Pufang, founder of the China Disabled Persons' Federation, and me in 2001. He is a member of our International Board of Advisors (see story page 127).

A kiss for a wonderful young lady in China, 2004.

I am honored to meet wheelchair recipient Xie Yanhong of China, the first physically disabled man to swim the English Channel (see story page 131).

Meeting more wheelchair recipients in China, 2004. I give each one a hand-shake and a smile (see story page 128).

Kun Sha, a Chinese orphan, sang to me when he received
his wheelchair from us in 2002 (see story page 130).

Another distribution in China, where millions of people need a wheelchair but cannot afford one.

of any hope. After the wheelchair distribution, we went to a downtown market street, where we saw a young girl in one of our wheelchairs, which she had received several hours earlier. She smiled from ear to ear when she saw us. She told us that this was the first time she had ever been able to come to the market street. She was very happy, and even happier that she got another chance to thank us.

Romania

On a distribution in Romania, we went to a senior citizens' facility. All 480 residents were basically immobile. The facility had only four wheelchairs for their use. One of the wheelchairs was riding on metal rims without tires. Most of these people spend their senior years lying in bed. When put into a wheelchair, they cried and looked at me with thanks; they grabbed my hands and prayed for me. One woman held my hand until an interpreter came. She proudly told me that she was 96 years old. "My eyes are not good, but I can see a little," she said. "My ears are not good, but I can hear a little. And now, thanks to you, I can move a little. I think I will live 10 more years."

We did not speak the same language, but we understood we had helped give them a new reason to live and hope.

The Ukraine

Rotarian Tom Venable learned the joy of giving wheelchairs in the city of Belaya Tserkov. A resident, Alexander Kosayk, was unable to walk and was confined to either a bed or chair for most of the day while his wife, Lena, worked as a taxi dispatcher. Tom, a member of the Rotary Club of Thousand Oaks, California, showed up at the Kosayk apartment with a distribution team. The couple was so moved that Lena presented Tom with the sole wall decoration in the apartment, a small plaque of an angel she had made herself.

"No one in the world has enough money to buy this plaque from me," Tom said later. "It is a priceless reminder of how precious the gift of mobility truly is."

In the Ukraine, with 47 million people, a million people remain in need of wheelchairs. There are an estimated one million land mines and pieces of unexploded ordnance in the country left over from World War II. Fifty percent of the victims each year are reported to be children.

Turkey

I have had the opportunity to meet with His All Holiness Ecumenical Patriarch Bartholomew, spiritual leader of the Greek Orthodox Church, on three occasions. At a distribution in Istanbul (known to the Greeks as Constantinople), we delivered wheelchairs at church headquarters and at a rehabilitation center outside of the city. I enjoyed learning about the Greek Orthodox faith, as I enjoy learning about other world religions. I also joined His Holiness on a trip to Cuba for the dedication of the first church built there since President Fidel Castro came to power. In Cuba, we held wheelchair distributions and enjoyed having dinner two nights in a row with His Holiness, President Castro and the former king and queen of Greece. In the future, we look forward to working with the church to deliver wheelchairs in many parts of the world.

Russia

Russia

We want to help physically disabled people in Russia, where an estimated 500,000 land mines and pieces of unexploded ordnance remain in the ground, mainly from World War II. Many other people are disabled by injury, disease or old age.

We were able to deliver a limited number of wheelchairs to Russia in association with Mikhail Gorbachev, the former president of the Soviet Union. I met him through the Academy of Achievement. After I got to know him, he agreed to become a member of our International Board of Advisors.

One of the ongoing challenges of distributing wheelchairs in Russia is the steep duties on foreign-made medical equipment. To overcome this obstacle, we have recently begun working with the Russian government; we agreed to have wheelchairs designated for and built in Russia, with a government subsidy to help keep costs low. To help our mission in Russia, I traveled to Moscow in 2003 with former Utah Governor Mike Leavitt. We met the mayor of the city and visited Moscow University. Through our Rotarian partners and Sister Cities International, we delivered wheelchairs to Dubna, Russia, that year.

Middle East

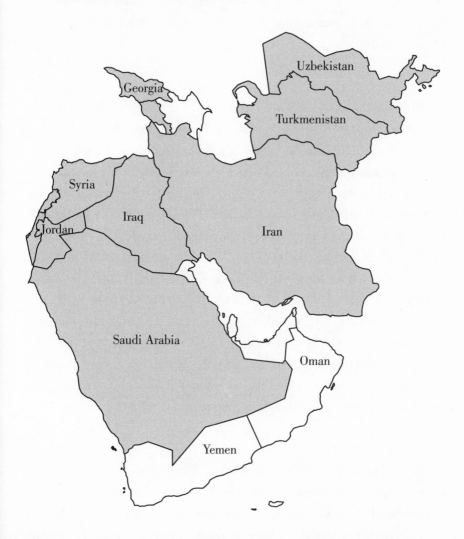

We have been delivering wheelchairs in this vital region of the world since 2000. We have sent many to Israel, and we brought wheelchairs to the Palestinian Territories, Egypt, Iran, Iraq, Jordan, Syria, Lebanon and other destinations. Many wheelchairs brought to the region are labeled with a patch that reads, "Given in Friendship

from the People of the United States." In 2004, we announced a
Middle East Initiative, in partnership with the U.S. Department of
State and U.S. Department of Defense, to ensure that this important
mission continues.

Iraq

Iraq is a country of 25 million people that has been devastated
by dictatorship, war and ethnic unrest. In December 2003, 10
months after the liberation of Iraq, the Foundation's first container of
280 wheelchairs was received by Life for Relief & Development, a
non-governmental organization working in partnership with the newly
established Iraqi Handicapped Society. The shipment was sponsored
by Rotarians in the United States and Canada, and was transported
by the U.S. Department of Defense. Wheelchairs were distributed to
physically disabled Iraqis in Baghdad, Karbala and Tikrit; they rep-
resented the first of four containers sponsored by Rotarians en route
to Iraq at the time. Among other challenges in Iraq, experts estimated that there are nearly seven million land mines separating the
Kurdish north from southern Iraq, and the number of people being
injured by land mines in this region is among the highest in the
world. In northern Iraq, about one person a day steps on a mine.

Iran

On a distribution in Iran in 2003, a Wheelchair Foundation
team member saw a disabled man in downtown Tehran who had
leather sandals on his hands. When the team member offered him a
wheelchair, the man said, "Are you telling me the truth?" The team
member said "Yes," and he started to cry. He said no one ever
talked to him or paid any attention to him at all. After we gave him
a wheelchair, representatives from the Persian Center, a U.S. nonprofit organization dedicated to helping the Iranian people, gave
him some money and told him that they valued him as a human

being. The man responded with great thanks and told them they had touched his heart as no one ever had.

Gaza Strip

The Wheelchair Foundation celebrated the new year in 2001 by bringing the gift of mobility to Palestinian people in the Gaza Strip. By distributing desperately needed wheelchairs to people of all ages just outside of Gaza City, Foundation workers and a team of volunteer physical and occupational therapists sent a message of hope to the area and highlighted the fact that human need knows no borders.

The group worked in partnership with the Palestinian Children's Relief Fund and other local charities to distribute wheelchairs through the Society of Physically Handicapped People of Gaza. Within the Gaza Strip, which is sandwiched between Egypt and Israel, an estimated 30,000 people, many of whom are refugees, need wheelchairs, according to Dr. Sameer Z. Abu Jayyab, executive chairman of the Society. Few of the 1.1 million residents can afford wheelchairs, as the densely populated area has suffered greatly from the recent conflict in the region. Some experts estimate unemployment as high as 65 percent, and the average resident lives on less than $3 per day.

Working under the shadow of violence and even the occasional rumble of nearby explosions, the team sought to aid the innocent and spread hope and healing amid the rubble of war. We teamed with Los Angeles-based Wheels for Humanity to provide refurbished wheelchairs in Gaza City. One man, who had once lived in America and had returned to Gaza, had been searching for six years to find a wheelchair for his daughter. Grateful, he said the Foundation was able to provide his eight-year-old girl a gift that no local governmental or charitable group had been able to give her. Mohammed, a 10-year-old boy with spina bifida, had lived his life on the ground. In his new wheelchair, he was eager to explore. And from miles around, elderly women carried in on blankets and aged men hoisted on wooden planks came to our distribution. They were among the many people in the large room the team used to fit individuals into wheelchairs. In one family alone, immobile twin men and their young sister left the room smiling in new wheelchairs.

A Foundation team returned to Gaza in September 2001 for another delivery. It distributed wheelchairs from the lobby of the Palestine Hotel in Gaza City and later at a hospital in Hebron.

Israel

Just outside of Tel Aviv in 2001, a delivery team distributed wheelchairs at the Assaf Harofeh Medical Center. Half of the donated wheelchairs were refurbished and specially designed to assist children with spinal curvature problems. These wheelchairs were sent to the Center's Special Pediatric Rehabilitative Unit and School. The other half of the wheelchairs were distributed throughout the Center and were particularly useful in its geriatric ward. "We never imagined in our wildest dreams that we would get such great wheelchairs," said Dr. Mordechai Waron, former director of the Medical Center, who attended the event.

Dr. Waron pointed to one young man moving himself in his new wheelchair. "This wonderful child, he was never so happy and never so mobile and never so active in his life like in the last few hours."

The donation was sorely needed, according to Erica Reiter, of the California-based Friends of Assaf Harofeh, which helps raise funds for the Israeli hospital. "Even with limited funds for equipment, the hospital serves some of the poorest people in Israel and is in an area with one of the fastest growing populations," Reiter said. "Because the demand for these wheelchairs is much greater than the supply, the Wheelchair Foundation's gift is a much-needed boost for the hospital."

Jordan

Seeking to bring relief and hope to residents in Amman, the Foundation teamed up with the Al-Hussein Society to deliver 240 wheelchairs in 2001. The wheelchairs went to a rehabilitation center for the physically challenged established by the late King Hussein and Queen Noor. The center serves many young children. One of the recipients, a young boy, grinned from ear to ear as he talked about how much he liked his "bicycle." Though not a bike in any traditional sense, the boy's new wheelchair did give him a means to get outside, to race with other boys, to go exploring and to go to school. The "Seventh Circle Man," a 40-year-old who for years had to crawl around the Seventh Circle, a busy Amman intersection, now has a wheelchair. Family and friends no longer have to worry about him being run over because he has to crawl in traffic. Other recipients included a 10-year-old girl who lost control of her limbs after being stricken with meningitis and a 20-year-old man with no use of his arms and with only one leg, who painted a picture with his toes of the two Americans who presented him a wheelchair.

"I am very thankful for the Wheelchair Foundation because of the opportunities given to children," said Jordanian Princess Majda Raad, who runs the Al-Hussein Society. "The gift of a new wheelchair gives our children the gift of a new perspective and lets them experience and explore their environment." The wheelchair deliveries in Amman were made possible by the Rotary Club of Woodside/Portola Valley, California.

We went back to Jordan twice in 2004. As part of one trip, we returned to Amman to give more wheelchairs to the rehabilitation center. We were met at the airport by a delegation of Jordanian Rotarians, who have been very committed to getting wheelchairs distributed throughout the country. I had been to the center so many times that the children there know me now. I am proud that we have been able to help give them freedom and mobility with our wheelchairs.

Saudi Arabia

Saudi Arabia has a foundation dedicated to helping the physically disabled. We have recently entered into an agreement with the Saudis to help the immobile of their country who cannot afford to purchase a wheelchair. In 2004, I met in Riyadh with Prince Sultan Bin Salman Bin Abdulaziz, the famous Saudi who orbited the Earth in the space shuttle. He is chairman of the Prince Sultan Center for Disability Research. I took wheelchairs with me for the physically disabled children at the center. The director told me, "We want to be part of your effort. Our work is the same." I also visited the Prince Sultan Humanitarian City.

After our meeting, the prince invited our delegation to a traditional banquet at his home in the desert. The next night, we found ourselves sitting on beautiful carpets, dining under the palms, discussing how we could work together to deliver wheelchairs in his country.

Lebanon

A Wheelchair Foundation team and several sponsors, including Dr. Joe Zeiter of Stockton, California, went to Lebanon to distribute wheelchairs in 2001. First Lady Andree Lahoud participated in the deliveries and agreed to become a member of the Wheelchair Foundation's International Board of Advisors and to assist in future distributions in the region. Among other stops, the team distributed wheelchairs at a Palestinian refugee camp in southern Lebanon. The trip took the team members through both Lebanese and Palestinian military checkpoints and past dozens of unmarked mine fields. They visited a privately funded clinic in the camp that was established by the United Nations in 1948. It serves 80,000 refugees living in an area of approximately 160 square acres. There are thousands of physically disabled people in the camp who need a wheelchair.

At one point, a woman recipient began to cry for joy. She could not believe she was actually receiving a wheelchair. Suddenly, her 10-year-old daughter ran up and started hitting the team members adjusting the footrests. She thought they were hurting her mother, because she had never seen her cry before. When her mother explained to her what was happening, the girl's look changed to one of gratitude and apology. The moment brought tears to the eyes of many members of the gathered crowd.

United States

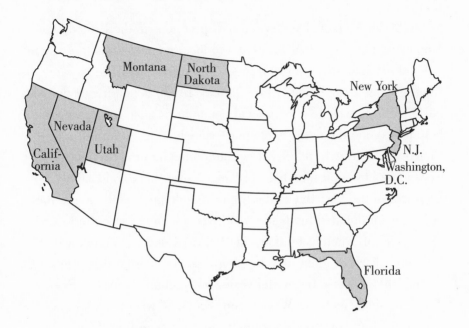

We have not limited our work to countries outside of the United States. We have Wheelchair Foundation offices in California, Florida, Las Vegas, New York City and Washington, D.C. To date, we have donated more than 17,000 wheelchairs in America.

We began delivering wheelchairs across the United States with the Salvation Army in 2000 and distributed wheelchairs to senior citizens at the Crow Indian Nation in Montana. The Oakland A's baseball organization and one of its owners, my friend Ken Hofmann, and other sponsors provided wheelchairs to people in Oakland, California. Rotarians and Major League Baseball sponsored wheelchairs in New York and New Jersey that were distributed by Goodwill Industries and Catholic Charities. The late builder Ralph Englestad and his wife, Betty, agreed to sponsor wheelchairs for every needy person in North Dakota and Nevada. Led by Mike

Leavitt when he was governor of Utah, several sponsors agreed to help us eliminate immobility in Utah, and we recently began that program.

In 2004, we launched several new programs in the United States. We began giving sports wheelchairs to local organizations throughout the country in association with the U.S. Paralympics. The International Association of Firefighters (IAFF) is helping us deliver basic mobility wheelchairs to local communities and has agreed to help us expand the delivery of sports wheelchairs. At an event in Concord, California, in 2004, the Foundation and the firefighters were joined by representatives of Wells Fargo Bank and Catholic Charities of the East Bay to distribute wheelchairs. Wells Fargo Bank of Rossmoor donated funds to provide wheelchairs in Contra Costa County, 30 of which were distributed at the Concord ceremony. Catholic Charities identified the recipients and hosted the event.

In 2004, we also began delivering wheelchairs to Walter Reed Army Medical Center in Washington, D.C. The wheelchairs went mainly to help amputees returning from the war in Iraq. While we were making arrangements to deliver the regular wheelchairs, we found out that there was a gymnasium that patients were encouraged to use. We delivered 10 sports wheelchairs to the gym for wheelchair basketball games. Our friend Jim Teetzel of Wilcox Industries, a government contractor, helped sponsor the wheelchairs. Disabled Sports USA and the U.S. Paralympics teams have visited the hospital on several occasions to show injured soldiers that sports can still be fun and rewarding, despite injuries.

Of course many of our terrific partners, donors and volunteers come from the United States. Their stories are uplifting, too.

Inspired by Miguel Tejada, the former Oakland A's shortstop known for his grand slams, Justin Gonsalves, age 17, made a grand slam of his own in 2002. Justin, a Boy Scout, was a senior at Logan High School in Union City, California, when he attended an A's game and saw video footage of the team distributing wheelchairs in the Dominican Republic with the Wheelchair Foundation. He immediately decided to do something for the physically disabled as his Eagle Scout project.

After meeting with his troop leader, he planned a pancake breakfast fundraiser and a direct mail and outreach campaign to his community. One of the key requirements for his community service badge was to complete a minimum of 100 hours of community work. Justin could receive credit for each hour worked individually, as well as each hour of community service given by friends and family. He pulled together a team and logged more than 130 hours of service while raising $8,328.49 for the Foundation.

"It feels good to be a Boy Scout and help disabled people like this," Justin said. "It makes me even prouder to be a Scout." Justin's donation enabled the Foundation to deliver 111 wheelchairs to physically disabled people in Mexico. He participated in the distribution, changing many lives—including his own.

Latin and South America

We discovered an overwhelming need for wheelchairs in Mexico, Central and South America and the islands of the Caribbean. LDS Charities and the Rotarians are our most active "hands-on" partners in those countries. Here are some of the stories from our distributions there.

Honduras

In Honduras, we met a woman who had been a journalism student when she was hit by a truck 11 years earlier. She was 31 years old when we met her and had been confined to her bed since the accident. We gave her a wheelchair. The next day, she returned to tell us that she had re-enrolled in journalism school and was going to start class the following day. The gift of a wheelchair allowed her to resume her life.

At another distribution, a lady came in requesting a wheelchair. She had two children with her who had cerebral palsy. Three weeks earlier, her husband had had a stroke. She said if she could just get one wheelchair, she could use it for all three of them. She was overwhelmed with emotion when we insisted that she receive at least two wheelchairs for her family.

Nicaragua

In 2001, I traveled to Nicaragua with our friends from the LDS Church. We met a physically disabled nun. Two LDS members picked her up and placed her in a wheelchair. She remarked that she never imagined the LDS Church would help her, a Catholic, so that she could continue to devote her life to people in need.

Bolivia

In 2002, with the help of First Lady Virginia Gillum De Quiroga, we delivered wheelchairs in Bolivia with our partners at LDS Charities. Were it not for a nun who made it her life's work to rescue severely disabled orphans, two of the children who received wheelchairs that day might never have made it. One had been abandoned near death when she was just a few days old. The other, an eight-year-old boy, lost his mother during childbirth and was abandoned by his alcoholic father just one week prior to the distribution. They were both taken in by the nun and her orphanage.

With their new wheelchairs, the children received some independence and the ability to go where they wanted. These children, who had been left lying in the street, could now move about and see things that were once out of their reach. Mobility for them and other physically disabled orphans who received wheelchairs was also an answer to the sister's prayer. Because the children with wheelchairs could now interact freely among themselves, she could spend more time with others who needed help.

Paraguay

Foundation team members at an LDS Charities distribution ceremony organized by First Lady Susana Gaillide de Gonzalez Macci and her foundation, Fundación Primera Dama de la Nación, gave a wheelchair to a nine-year-old boy who had fallen from a roof when he was one year old. As soon as he received his wheelchair, he zoomed around the room, acting out his dream of playing basketball in the Paralympics.

The team also met Jorge, a 35-year-old father of two children who had lost his legs to gangrene 10 years earlier and had depended on his wife to provide for their family. Jorge said having a wheelchair made him feel like a man again, because now he could go back to work and once again provide for his family.

Guatemala

In 2003, my son David, president of the Wheelchair Foundation, celebrated his 25th college reunion with 13 classmates. These graduates of the Princeton University class of 1977 decided to travel to Guatemala to deliver wheelchairs to 240 physically disabled people. Princeton alumni are known for making a difference in America and around the world. They have long incorporated community service projects into their class reunions. Previous projects had been local; David wanted to see the class broaden its efforts. All of David's classmates loved the idea of delivering wheelchairs in Central America. They further expanded the scope of the project by adding educational and medical supplies to the delivery.

Coordinating the trip sparked a spirit of teamwork and unity among the classmates. While groups of graduates in San Francisco, Boston, Indianapolis and Washington, D.C., collected and packed 287 boxes of educational and medical supplies, the 14-member delivery team coordinated flight schedules and last-minute details—including efforts to fulfill a request for basketballs from a Guatemalan teacher, made less than 24 hours before the distribution team departed. Thanks to the use of my plane, no one had to worry about lost supplies, traveling alone or juggling flight schedules. On departure day, David loaded the supplies and flew to Dallas to meet his classmates.

Anticipation filled the air as alums greeted one another at the airport and learned that together they had already collected 17 basketballs! Each classmate was eager to share his or her talents. Some would share their medical skills by volunteering in hospitals and health clinics. Others would share their skills as Spanish teachers by volunteering in local schools, working with children and serving as translators. All of the team members shared compassionate hearts.

Within minutes of their arrival, the team set up in a hotel room and began unpacking and re-sorting supplies so that they would be ready for three days of visits. Team members stuffed pens, pencils, rulers, scissors and crayons into black and orange backpacks; each one was handmade by a classmate to match Princeton's colors. Other alumni assembled kits containing soap, brushes, toothbrushes, toothpaste, towels and washcloths. These were combined with prepackaged personal hygiene kits and USA Track and Field hats, shorts and socks contributed by classmate Craig Masback and blankets and robes contributed by LDS Charities.

Before dawn on the first day, the wheelchair team had already started on a five-hour journey to Coban, known as "the end of the paved road." Many of the recipients had crawled or been carried an hour or more from their villages to get to the distribution site. Alumnus Ron Petrowski, whose 15-year-old son with muscular dystrophy is confined to a wheelchair, was particularly moved. And since he is fluent in Spanish, he was able to hear the stories of several of the recipients.

"Ron was able to hold their hands, hear their stories and truly relate to their experience in a way that none of the rest of us could," David said later.

The team met an elderly man who was clearly worn down by years of immobility. The man proudly wore a cowboy hat that seemed to reflect the dignity he felt in finally being able to move on his own. Fighting back tears, he said, "You'll never know what this means to me."

Equally moving was the story of an elderly woman who finally received an answer after 30 years of daily prayer for mobility. "You are sent from heaven," she said. "God is looking out for me."

Team members also distributed wheelchairs at a Presidential Palace ceremony hosted by the first lady of Guatemala, Evelyn De Portillo. At the event, team members met Marina, a beautiful five-year-old girl whose entire family was hit by a drunk driver. The accident killed her father and three siblings and left Marina paralyzed from the waist down. Though she looked very grown up in her Sunday best, the moment Marina was seated in her wheelchair, her face filled with wide-eyed wonder and delight. Almost instantly, she took off across the room, bubbling with excitement. Team members shared her happiness as they realized that Marina could now move herself and go wherever she wanted.

In all, 100 wheelchairs were distributed at the Presidential Palace, while another 20 wheelchairs were given to elderly residents at Hogar Geriatrica Maria, a retirement home. A number of residents have Alzheimer's. Without crutches, walkers or wheelchairs, many of them had been confined to their beds for years. Now they were able to get around the facility and enjoy the outdoors as well. In addition to the wheelchairs, the team supplied the residents with towels, robes and blankets.

Just before leaving, the medical team requested a wheelchair for Rosa Carlota Flores de Gonzalez, an 81-year-old great-great-great-grandmother. The team members determined that she would someday lose her leg at the hip. Forty years earlier, she had had a steel bar placed inside of her knee, which had been damaged by a tumor. She'd had to stay in bed for a year to recover. During that time, she started writing. She published four novels under the pseudonym Flor Marchita Entre Ruines (Withered Flower in the Ruins). That name so accurately describes how many people feel when they are immobile. When the team brought her wheelchair, Rosa was so surprised that she said it had "fallen from the air." With the wheelchair, Rosa could feel alive again, not as if she was lying in the ruins.

Altogether, the class of '77 raised $70,000 for wheelchairs, medicine and scholarships. Within three days, the team delivered 2,500 backpacks of school supplies, established five scholarships, distributed $5,000 worth of medical supplies to three medical facilities, handed out 200 personal hygiene kits and brought the gift of mobility to 240 people.

"We hope to set this as a benchmark for the reunion community service projects," David said. "This was one project where you really felt like you made an impact."

Peru

In 2003, LDS Charities joined us on a trip to Peru and three other South American countries. In Peru, we met with First Lady Eliane Karp, a naturalized U.S. citizen and Stanford University graduate, to deliver the first of 544 wheelchairs designated for that country. They were distributed at a ceremony at the National Petroleum Building.

We were moved by the story of Gloria, who struggled with declining bone density. She broke or cracked numerous bones as people moved her from place to place. Gloria was grateful for her new wheelchair, which enabled her to move about on her own and assist her family in the marketplace. Our team offered her a second wheelchair for her 25-year-old daughter, who suffered from a similar condition. Gloria refused. She said that she would share her wheelchair with her daughter so that another family could be blessed.

"Seeing the humility and gratitude expressed was a beacon to my soul," said Michelle Inkley, a senior analyst for LDS Charities and translator for the team. "Giving these people a wheelchair is giving them a life."

The Rotarians have also been very active in Peru. In 2002, members of the Rotary Club of North Colorado Springs helped sponsor a container of wheelchairs that traveled 2,500 miles up the Amazon River to Belén. Visiting Rotarians took some wheelchairs to homes where recipients were in frail health. One of the wheelchairs was destined for an elderly man of modest means, who was immobile from a stroke. A friend of the man took the delivery team in a car to his home. A local Rotarian hired a taxi to take the wheelchair and joined the team. The wheelchair gave the man a reason to look forward to a better life and made him very happy. A member of the team said afterward, "I don't know the words that will adequately describe the feeling we had when we brought a new life to this man in the form of a wheelchair. It is a wonderful thing when you can witness an immediate change in a person's hope for the future and receive a gift of gratitude that brought tears to our eyes."

Brazil

In 2000, I received a call from Queen Sofia of Spain, who asked me to deliver some wheelchairs to Brazil. She and King Juan Carlos were going to visit President Cardosa and First Lady Ruth Correa

Leite to celebrate Spain's great relationship with Brazil. I said I would be happy to come and asked when she wanted me. She said on Monday; it was already Thursday. I said I couldn't make the trip on such short notice but that I would air-express some wheelchairs. She said that was not what she wanted. She asked me to attend a distribution in Brazil in person. She said she would call back in two hours so I could give her my travel arrangements. I quickly learned that a queen is used to getting her way!

After my team scrambled to get visas and prepare a flight plan, I packed my plane with wheelchairs and took off for Brazil. We arranged to have a distribution at the Spanish embassy in the capital city, Brasilia. The king, queen, president and first lady helped with the delivery while a thousand VIP guests in formal attire waited two hours for the celebration to begin. I spoke with the Spanish ambassador, who had arranged and organized the ceremony. He said the event was the most difficult in his career! But at least 40 wheelchair recipients were happy—they each had a chance to meet the king and queen and their president and first lady.

On a Sunday afternoon in the capital, Foundation team members stopped at a local church and asked the priest if he knew of any people in the area who needed a wheelchair but could not afford one. He said yes, got into a car and led us into the countryside down red sandy roads. Team members arrived at a small cinderblock and tin shack. They were introduced to a family of eight. The family's "farm" had chickens and ducks in the yard, a single old swayback horse and a small garden. It had an open well with a bucket and rope for bringing up water. There wasn't much else. Team members were led into a single-room house, with one bed and some mats on the floor. In one corner was a large chair filled with rags. In it sat a girl with arms and legs as thin as fragile twigs. She had beautiful brown eyes and a very nice smile but couldn't speak. Her mother told the team that she was 18 years old and had been like this since birth. She lived in the chair and was unable to care for herself.

The team put her in the wheelchair and adjusted the leg rests to accommodate her withered limbs. Soon her sisters began wheeling her around the yard. The girls laughed and smiled. They told team members that they liked the wheelchair because it meant that they wouldn't have to carry their sister everywhere anymore. They were also excited because they could take her to more places with them. Her father, who had been talking with the priest, knelt down with him and they prayed. When they finished the prayer, the father came and thanked the team.

"Today is my birthday," he said. "This very morning I got up and asked God for one gift for my birthday, for someone to help my daughter. This Sunday, God sent you to me for my birthday. I thanked the Lord and I thank you."

Panama

In 2001, I went to Panama as a member of the board of the Smithsonian Institution. I decided to also deliver wheelchairs while I was there.

We worked with Panamanian President Mireya Elisa Moscoso Rodriguez and First Lady Moscoso de Young to deliver 240 wheelchairs to physically disabled people in Panama. In a whirlwind tour of the isthmus, we brought hope and mobility to people from ages 1 to 96, in addition to presenting other humanitarian goods to the first lady's foundation.

I took the president's plane to David, Panama, where I visited a hospital for the critically disabled, people who had been abandoned by their families. With wheelchairs, at least some of them could be moved outside to sit in the sun. I also visited the Mother Theresa of Calcutta Orphanage to deliver specialized wheelchairs to each of the orphanage's 18 children with cerebral palsy. In the city of Colon, a 70-year-old man who could not afford a wheelchair broke down, crying in gratitude when I gave him one. The first lady was deeply moved by the experience.

"The work and generosity of the Wheelchair Foundation has changed the lives of so many of my country's people," she said. "I was so moved and inspired to see the results of the Foundation's donation and to personally help those who received wheelchairs. Panama is very grateful for the Foundation's work."

Puerto Rico

In 2003, I accompanied Jacalyn Leavitt, the former first lady of Utah, on a distribution in San Juan. In a report in our newsletter, *Changing the World*, Jacalyn wrote that the experience made "my heart sing." She helped give a wheelchair to a boy named Angel, who suffered from a debilitating disease that tightens and pulls his ligaments inward, distorting his body. Though he was small and frail for a boy of 13, she said she knew he had the same wants and needs as her healthy 13-year-old son. Angel's ailment robbed him of the dignity and independence teenagers so desperately want. His new wheelchair gave him some of that independence. Angel responded to the wheelchair by quickly placing his hands on the wheels and experiencing a great sense of satisfaction at his newfound mobility. He immediately began to maneuver himself about, very proud to show his mother and all of us the empowerment he had been given.

Colombia

Our Rotary friends delivered wheelchairs in Colombia in early 2004. Frank Dean, assistant governor of Rotary District 7670 in North Carolina, is a former lieutenant colonel in the U.S. Army. He met a man who had lost a leg when he stepped on a land mine. When Frank asked the man if he was a soldier, the man replied, "Yes." Frank presented the man with his wheelchair, saying, "From one soldier to another soldier, I want you to accept this wheelchair as my gift to you."

"It was like I had said something divine," Frank recalled. "The look on that man's face was priceless. It was a tender moment. This might have been the crowning moment of my life. When you can experience this firsthand, it is truly amazing."

An estimated 100,000 land mines and pieces of unexploded ordnance exist in Columbia, a country of 42 million people. It is the only country in the Americas where land mines are being actively buried, by antigovernment forces.

Mexico

Second to China, we have delivered more wheelchairs in Mexico than in any other country. Its shared border with the United States makes deliveries there easier to attend for Rotary Clubs sponsoring hands-on service projects.

I joined Rotarians from northern California to deliver 240 wheelchairs at a small soccer stadium in Texcoco, outside of Mexico City, in 2001. The population of the city and its surrounding area is 25 million people. It is estimated that 1.2 million Mexicans need a wheelchair but cannot afford one.

One of them was Martina Miranda, age 42, who had been physically disabled by polio. She told our Rotary friends that she'd had a wheelchair about 20 years earlier. It lasted only five years and she could not afford another one. To get to the bus each morning, her nephew wheeled her on a hand truck as she sat on a milk crate. She worked at a roadside stand selling shoe polish. Other times, she walked on her knees. Her 85-year-old mother had lifted and helped her for the past 42 years. They had tears of joy in their eyes when they received her wheelchair. Martina said, "I have prayed so long for another wheelchair, and I knew that my prayers would be answered." Her mother said that they could never have afforded such a beautiful wheelchair and that the gift would make the remaining years of her life much easier.

Martina told us that 10 years earlier, she thought she would get another wheelchair. A man had told her he could get her a wheelchair from the government free of charge if she just paid the shipping. It was a scam. She lost 70 pesos (less than $8.00 at the time). It was all the money her family could scrape together over three months. This is just one example of the stories we hear from people who need a wheelchair but cannot afford one. (As we were leaving, a member of the Rotary team handed Martina's mother 200 pesos, about $20, to make up for the money lost to the con man.)

At a distribution in Mexico City, a man in his 70s arrived with his wife. He had diabetes and had lost both legs and was blind in one eye. He had a wheelchair, but it was old and often fell apart. When his wheelchair would break, the man would sometimes be injured in the fall. His illness made him more vulnerable to injury; the falls caused huge bumps on his head, bruises on his ribs and scrapes all over his body. His new wheelchair not only gave him better mobility, it gave him protection from falls.

Another Mexico City recipient was a three-year-old girl who had been wheeled around in a baby stroller. When the girl, named Lady, got too big for the stroller, her mother carried her in a sling. This put strain on the mother's back and limited their activities. Lady received her wheelchair and quickly learned to move around on her own for the first time in her life. Her mother said, "The wheelchair gives me freedom to take Lady with me wherever I go."

A third recipient was Alejandro, a man in his mid-40s. He had been in a serious car wreck several years earlier and lost his legs. After his accident, he did not travel outside of his town in the mountains. When he heard about the wheelchair distribution, a friend hired a taxi that drove two hours from the town to Mexico City. Alejandro received a wheelchair and returned to his home a mobile man.

A fourth recipient was Lizzy, who traveled four hours to get to the distribution. She had been paralyzed from a serious surgery after birth. She received a wheelchair and "stole the show"—she never stopped smiling for the entire hour-and-a-half event.

Jon Grant, who has been an ambassador between Rotarians worldwide and the Foundation, along with his wife, Linda, continues to do important work in Mexico, especially with young people from the United States. In recent distributions there, he has taken high school students from California with him.

"They come from comfortable lives in the U.S., not realizing that not everyone in the world has cell phones and computers and TVs," Jon said. "They get to help somebody less fortunate and they realize that one person can really make a difference. They learn that by working together, their efforts are changing people's lives."

One of my most memorable distribution stories involves a woman named Maria, who has worked for my family for more than a decade. When she heard that we were going to Mexico City, she told me she had a nephew there who had lost his eyesight and mobility because of a terminal disease. She asked if we could give him a wheelchair so that he could be mobile during the time he had left. I said, "Of course," and asked her to arrange getting him to our distribution.

His parents found us the day of the event. Through tears of gratitude they said Angel had received his wheelchair and wanted to thank me. They brought him to me and I took his hands and spoke to him so he would know where I was. Then he grasped my hands, turned his blind eyes toward my eyes and said, "I will see you in heaven." He touched me so deeply that I was not able to answer him.

* * *

Since we launched the Wheelchair Foundation, we have given away nearly 300,000 wheelchairs, and behind every one of them is a story like the ones you have just read. Yet we have a lot of work left to do. The World Health Organization estimates that more than 25 million people around the globe are immobile. But based on our firsthand experience, we believe the number is actually 3 percent of the world's population, or as many as 190 million people. Giving all of them wheelchairs will be a huge undertaking and will cost billions of dollars.

But I feel there is no choice. In most cases, we are helping people who have no dignity, no hope, no future. Then suddenly, with the gift of a wheelchair, they feel as though they have become part of the human race. They now have pride, they now have hope. They may not be able to do everything they want, but at least they will be able to be more independent, to open a milk bar, go back to school, splash in a fountain or just sit in the sun.

We cannot forget how much the gift of a wheelchair can also help family members and caregivers: parents who no longer have to carry a child everywhere, siblings who no longer have to pick up a heavy brother or sister. In many cases, a wheelchair gives them freedom, too—freedom to get a job or education, to get out of the house more, to live a fuller life.

But we need your help. Every wheelchair changes a life. What a simple way to give *purpose* to *your* life.

Chapter 10:
FINDING YOUR PURPOSE

The purpose of life is a life of purpose.

Robert Byrne

In April 2003, I received an e-mail from "a cripple in China." That's not the way we talk of the disabled in the United States, but those were the words Zou Xiaoliang used to describe himself to me. We had given him a wheelchair in March 2002. He had contracted polio at age one. People carried him on their backs from place to place; on the ground, he moved with the help of a small stool. But a wheelchair changed his life.

"Sitting on the wheelchair and driving its wheels, I seem to grow a pair of wings," he said in his note. "By wheelchair, I go to library to find more information I never knew before. By wheelchair, I visit some translation service to get chances for supporting my life. By wheelchair, I spend some of my spare time in parks to enjoy fresh air and beautiful sight."

"Thousands and thousands of words just come into one," he continued. "Thanks."

No, Xiaoliang, the thanks are all mine. Just as I helped physically challenged people change their lives by giving them wheelchairs, giving wheelchairs to them helped change my life. Incredible, inspiring people like Zou Xiaoliang helped me find my purpose. They helped me find joy.

How do you find your purpose? Very simple: Open your heart and listen to your heart. It's not hard. Try it right now: Can you feel in your heart if something is missing in your life? Do you feel incomplete? Do you have all the material possessions you want but still feel unfulfilled, feel no joy? Then that is a powerful clue that you have not found your purpose—and that you need to start looking for it. That's the way I felt for most of my life.

I don't know why I do some of the things I do. I just do them. Something affects me and I react. To find your purpose, ask yourself, What affects me? What breaks my heart when I see it? What strikes a nerve? Then follow that feeling to some course of action. Once you act, if you feel a sense of joy, of pleasure, of satisfaction, a feeling you have never felt before, then you have found your purpose.

Duty is not purpose. Many people do things out of a sense of duty. I helped my parents financially later in life because, as their son, it was my duty. Many people give money to charitable causes because they think it is their duty, "the right thing to do," or for recognition—not because of any pleasure they get from it. That's okay, because that helps a lot of charities raise money for good causes. But to me, it's a shame. If you're looking for recognition or approval from others, your donation is not really a gift. You're trying to buy something. I say this not to be critical but to try to inspire others to look beyond their own wants—something that took me almost a lifetime to do. I've since learned that my greatest joy has come from giving without expecting anything in return. Even if the only thing you get back is your own satisfaction, nothing compares with the feeling of knowing that someone else's life is a little better because of your effort. My greatest regret is that it took me most of my life to figure this out.

It's hard for me to ever feel any real contentment, because I am never satisfied. For every person that we help, there are millions more in need. I see millions of arms reaching up. The real legacy I hope to leave is to get more people helping other people, so that after I'm gone, the work I've done will continue to multiply. I'm constantly learning about new areas of need and new opportunities to improve lives of people less fortunate.

One area of need is clean water. In many countries I've traveled to, water pollution is a major problem. Now I am working with a company that's developing proprietary water purification technology. It will produce pure drinking water from virtually any source while using 40 times less energy than traditional purification systems. The equipment is light and portable—only 110 pounds—so that it can be moved quickly to any place it's needed. Can you imagine the impact this technology could have on people in developing nations?

Why stop there? I envision a group of the world's biggest philan-thropists and their organizations coming together. We could unite in common goals. I would love nothing more than to see the group establish centers in all countries, particularly third-world countries, that could help disseminate chairs, training and education for the disabled. But it could, and should, try to meet as many human needs as possible. For example, these same centers could provide vaccines for any and all diseases. They could provide eye surgery, orthopedic operations, dentistry and other minor operations.

Mostly volunteer doctors, dentists and nurses would staff these "Headquarters of Hope," as I like to call them. They could use vaca-tion time to serve the needy and train people in countries they visit in medicine, health care and advocacy. Think of it—the centers could dispense wheelchairs, hearing aids, blankets and all the other things given by churches, religious groups and so many other generous organizations. The centers could also help train people for entering the workforce and house development banks to give loans to people to start small businesses. They could provide schools in their communities with used textbooks, pencils and educational supplies. They would embrace all religious groups, all ages and races. Disabled people who were given a second chance in life could help staff them. Maybe the disabled could also play a role in transporting supplies to distant villages and settlements.

This effort could not only help people in general, it could help solve a major problem of our age: terrorism. The poor and disabled need to know there is hope, that there are people in the world who care about them. I've found that people respond to kindness—their attitude changes immediately if you give them help and respect. I truly believe that the road to peace in the world is through person-to-person goodwill, not the threat of war or negotiations among leaders.

Sounds like a tall order, doesn't it? But I believe anything is possible.

I started on my road to purpose with a wheelchair given to a man in Romania. Then I dreamed about possibilities. Now, more than four years later, the Wheelchair Foundation is an international organization that touches the lives of people, families and communities in more than 125 countries. The foundation now has its own life. It is helped by corporations, organizations, governments, nonprofit groups and, most important, by ordinary people from all parts of the world.

I like the life that I've created. I achieved great wealth in worldly goods in my eyes and in the eyes of the world. I achieved the ultimate dream of that poor boy from Wisconsin by owning my own jet, a football team, a large yacht, several large homes and a great classic car collection, and by traveling the world and associating with famous people. I felt I was indeed rich.

But in truth, I was neither fulfilled nor satisfied with my life. Something important was missing. I know now that I did not really know what being poor was—and I did not know what being rich was. On my road to purpose, I learned that I received joy from giving hope, freedom and dignity to some of the poorest, most unfortunate and forgotten people in the world. The most joy I've experienced has come from doing something good for someone else—especially when that person wasn't expecting it.

You don't have to be rich, own big houses or planes, travel or know famous people to do something good for someone else. You can start out small, like I did—with one wheelchair for one person, one act of kindness for one person, one smile for one person, maybe just once a month or with just 1 percent of your time. Who knows—perhaps you'll end up helping thousands of people, as I did.

With purpose like that, I believe we could change the world.

THE NEXT CHAPTER

As we develop the technology to turn undrinkable water into pure, healthy water, I feel that this potentially will change the lives of millions of people in poverty around the world and will prevent many diseases and disabilities.

I am still discovering **PURPOSE** in my life.

Appendix A:
"THE DO-ERS," OUR FRIENDS IN PARTNERSHIP

The Wheelchair Foundation works with many companies, foundations and organizations to distribute wheelchairs around the world. The Foundation is grateful for all of the financial and other support they provide for its mission and looks forwards to working with them for years to come.

Rotary Clubs and Rotarians
www.rotary.org

Since March 2001, Rotary Clubs, Districts and individual Rotarians have sponsored the delivery of more than 90,000 wheelchairs to more than 85 countries around the world. To date, Rotarians from every one of the 50 United States and every province of Canada have participated in the Wheelchair Foundation mission. Ken Behring is a member of the Rotary Club of Foster City, California.

Rotarians are a part of an organization that consists of 1.2 million business and professional leaders worldwide. They provide humanitarian service, encourage high ethical standards in their work and help build goodwill and peace in the world. There are some 31,000 Rotary Clubs in more than 160 countries. The Rotarians' motto is Service Above Self.

Over the past 20 years, Rotarians have contributed more than $500 million toward the worldwide eradication of polio and have coordinated National Immunization Days that have vaccinated up to

100 million people in a single day in India. The original vision of Rotarian leaders was to team up with the Wheelchair Foundation to deliver mobility to victims of polio that the vaccine can no longer help. It is estimated that to date the Wheelchair Foundation has delivered up to 100,000 wheelchairs to polio victims worldwide.

Some of the best reasons to be a member of a Rotary Club in North America are the heartwarming stories of friendship and gratitude that are brought back by members who have traveled abroad and participated in a hands-on humanitarian service project. But some of the realities that they face on these missions of peace are that disease, advanced age and accidents are the primary reasons for needing a wheelchair. But land mines and unexploded ordnance (UXO) continue to be a problem worldwide as a cause of physical disability. It is estimated that more than 60 million to 70 million land mines are planted in nearly 60 countries. And that number does not include the millions of UXOs that are left over from world wars and thousands of regional conflicts since the early 20th century.

In 2002, the Wheelchair Foundation, in conjunction with the U.S. Department of State and the U.S. Department of Defense, initiated a global outreach program to deliver wheelchairs to the victims of land mines and UXOs. Rotarians have participated in missions to the most land mine- and UXO-infested countries of the world, including Angola, Sierra Leone, Mozambique, Eritrea, Egypt, Iraq, Afghanistan, Bosnia, Croatia, Vietnam, Cambodia and Laos, among others. The Wheelchair Foundation is grateful for the dedicated efforts of Rotarians worldwide to expand the global reach of our mission.

The Church of Jesus Christ of Latter-day Saints
www.lds.org

The very first "Global Partner" in the Wheelchair Foundation's mission to bring hope, mobility and freedom into the lives of people with physical disabilities was The Church of Jesus Christ of Latter-day Saints.

The members of the LDS Church are building on a long and established tradition of compassion and charity by reaching out to help those who are in need of a better life. During the economic devastation of the Great Depression, the church formalized its present-day welfare program. The first president of the church initiated the emphasis of helping people to help themselves. The church then began a comprehensive program to provide food, employment, training and social services for those who need them.

"We've been directed by our Savior to love one another," said Bishop Attridge of Salt Lake City. "To lighten the burdens of one another, to lift the load, to help out. When people go out to do this, they can't help but feel good about themselves."

Each year, members volunteer hundreds of thousands of hours, on farms, in canneries, storehouses, and training facilities, to provide food for the hungry, relieve the pain of those who suffer and offer a helping hand to those who yearn to become more independent. And always, this is done in a way that brings joy to those who give, and fosters self-reliance for those who are in need.

The Humanitarian Services arm of The Church of Jesus Christ of Latter-day Saints (www.providentliving.org) was organized in 1985. Since the establishment of the Wheelchair Foundation in June 2000, the LDS Church has sponsored the delivery of tens of thousands of wheelchairs each year around the world. Combining hands-on wheelchair distributions with ongoing humanitarian programs in dozens of countries, young missionaries and senior couples working with local church members participate in multifaceted deliveries of clothing, food, medical supplies and vocational training as a small part of their global effort.

Touching and improving lives on every inhabited continent of the Earth regardless of race, color or creed is a common thread that exists effortlessly within the circle of partners that share the mission of the Wheelchair Foundation. The strength of our joined hands sends a message of peace, love and friendship to the world, and allows us to accelerate our humanitarian efforts on a daily basis. For this reason, we see the eradication of immobility as a reachable goal during the 21st century.

The Wheelchair Foundation expresses its most sincere thanks for the selfless commitment of The Church of Jesus Christ of Latter-day Saints to helping improve the quality of people's lives worldwide.

U.S. Department of State and U.S. Department of Defense
www.state.gov
www.dsca.mil

The Wheelchair Foundation has been working with support from the U.S. Department of State and the U.S. Department of Defense since 2002. As a result of the resources provided by the State and Defense Departments, the collaboration has already delivered more than 100,000 wheelchairs to more than 90 countries around the world. It works to bring hope, mobility and freedom to victims of disease, accidents, natural disasters and war. The collaboration serves as a model of American public/private partnerships working to help send the message of friendship and goodwill worldwide.

China Disabled Persons' Federation
www.cdpf.org.cn/english/about.htm

The CDPF represents more than 60 million people with various categories of disabilities in China, including the physically disabled. The organization's goals are to promote humanitarianism and to protect the human rights of persons with disabilities. It also ensures their equal participation in society, their contribution to economic growth and their social development, as well as their equal share in the material and culture achievements of China. CDPF has established chapters in most communities throughout the country. The Wheelchair Foundation has partnerships in 32 major cities in China, with both CDPF chapters and city governments.

According to the CDPF, rapid economic growth and social transformation in China have changed the environment for the disabled there. People no longer regard those with disabilities as "useless," recognizing that they are "equal creators" of material and spiritual wealth. Chinese society is giving more understanding, respect, concern and assistance to people with disabilities. Disabled people, in turn, now treasure their own worth as contributors to society in the spirit of self-respect, self-confidence, self-improvement and self-reliance. Disabled people's organizations in both rural and urban areas now vigorously protect the rights and interests of people with disabilities. Coordinating bodies on disability bring government agencies, disabled people's organizations and other social sectors together to work for the advancement of people with disabilities. At the same time, the government has promulgated legislation to protect the human rights of people with disabilities.

The work of the CDPF includes:

- Making contact with persons with disabilities, listening to their views and suggestions, reflecting their needs and serving them wholeheartedly.

- Uniting and encouraging persons with disabilities to abide by the law, perform their legal duties, carry an optimistic and up-and-coming attitude and develop a spirit of self-respect, self-confidence, self-improvement and self-reliance.

- Advocating the cause of persons with disabilities, facilitating the links among government officials, Chinese citizens and people with disabilities and mobilizing society to understand, respect, care for and assist people with disabilities.

- Developing and promoting rehabilitation, education, employment, cultural life, welfare and social service for persons with disabilities and the prevention of disabilities so as to improve the environment and conditions for the participation of persons with disabilities in society.

- Assisting government in studying, formulating and implementing disability-related laws, regulations, plans and programs, as well as in exercising its role in promoting, synthesizing, organizing, coordinating, consulting and providing services to the disabled, and in monitoring and guiding the work of the disabled.

- Carrying out international exchanges and cooperation.

The China Charity Federation

www.chinacharity.cn.net

The China Charity Federation (CCF) is a nationwide, nongovernmental charity organization. It was established in 1994 with the approval of the Chinese government; it is legally registered as an independent entity. Its members include individual citizens and social institutions interested in voluntary charitable work. The goal of CCF is to uphold the spirit of humanitarianism and the Chinese tradition of helping people in poverty or need, to help unfortunate individuals and groups of people and to conduct various kinds of social relief work.

Since its founding, CCF has also maintained its goal to promote public awareness of, and to broaden, charitable work in various fields in China. CCF's many projects have won it widespread recognition and the trust and full support of the government. CCF programs assist in disaster relief, poverty relief, medical care, care for senior citizens and orphans, help for teachers and students and help for the disabled. The Wheelchair Foundation has joined in a partnership with CCF called "Operation Mobility," which will solicit funds in China from companies and businesses for providing wheelchairs for the disabled.

Ministry of Civil Affairs of the People's Republic of China
www.mca.gov.cn

The Ministry of Civil Affairs develops the guiding principles, policies, laws, rules and regulations related to civil affairs. It is responsible for the work of giving social help, organizing and implementing programs to guarantee the minimum subsistence security of both urban and rural residents, organizing and directing efforts to alleviate poverty, helping the distressed and managing the activities of soliciting donations in relation to social welfare. It also oversees disaster relief, including organizing and coordinating disaster-relief work; organizing and directing the work of disaster-relief contributions and donations; and accepting, managing and distributing disaster-relief cash and materials. In addition, the ministry is responsible for the management of marriage and adoption of orphans. It also supports the Chinese army and veterans and family members of soldiers, officers and veterans.

Crystal Cathedral Ministries
www.crystalcathedral.org

The *Hour of Power* is broadcast from the beautiful Crystal Cathedral in Southern California, ministered by Dr. Robert H. Schuller, and his son, Dr. Robert A. Schuller. I have been a guest on the program twice. Those appearances have generated contributions to sponsor thousands of wheelchairs for the poor and physically disabled around the world. The Schullers' friendship and support have given me inspiration for our mission at the Foundation.

The Million Dollar Roundtable Foundation
www.mdrt.org

The Million Dollar Round Table (MDRT) is an association of the world's most successful life insurance and financial services professionals. In June 2003, I spoke at the MDRT's annual conference, stressing the worldwide need for wheelchairs and the hope, mobility and freedom a new wheelchair offers someone who, up to that point, had little, if any, hope.

My message was well received, and six months later the MDRT Foundation had sponsored containers of wheelchairs to different areas around the world.

Oakland Athletics
www.oaklandathletics.com

The Oakland Athletics Community Fund donated 4,200 wheelchairs to physically disabled residents of the Dominican Republic. This generosity has given children in that country the ability to go to school, adults the ability to provide for their families and a new lease on life for people suffering the effects of advanced age. The Oakland A's Community fund also supports charitable organizations in their efforts to improve education, aid the underprivileged, assist in crime and drug prevention and help children, seniors and those who work to improve the quality of life in the San Francisco Bay Area. The fund's programs include the Green Stampede Homework Club for at-risk youth; Home Run Readers, a literacy program; and A's Amigos for encouraging Hispanic youth. Ken Hofmann, who is a partner in the A's, has been instrumental in helping us and personally has donated funds to sponsor 1,600 wheelchairs for Italy and Mexico.

Knights of Columbus
www.kofc.org

The Knights of Columbus is a Catholic men's fraternal benefit society that was formed in 1882 to render financial aid to members and their families. The Knights sponsored 2,000 wheelchairs that were delivered to Afghanistan in 2003–2004, and thousands more worldwide. The wheelchairs are allowing some of the world's most physically devastated populations to send their children to school, their adults to work to provide for their families and their elderly to once again become a part of society. At Knights' councils, social and intellectual fellowship is promoted among members and their families through educational, charitable, religious, social welfare, war relief and public relief works. Bound together by the ideal of Christopher Columbus, the one whose hand brought Christianity to the New World, the Knights take charge in civic involvement and aid to those in need. Knights councils in California are taking the lead in spreading the word of our mission into their local communities and across the border into Mexico.

ChevronTexaco

www.chevrontexaco.com

ChevronTexaco takes pride not only in its products and services, but also in the way it conducts its worldwide operations. The company's principles and values are embodied in the ChevronTexaco Way, which provides an integrated framework for its strategies and goals, including its nonprofit activities. ChevronTexaco has sponsored the delivery of thousands of wheelchairs to the people of Angola. In this country of 12 million people, nearly 20 percent are immobile because of land mines, accidents and other causes. ChevronTexaco's dedication to helping people to help themselves in local communities has contributed greatly to the improvement of the quality of life for tens of thousands of people. Feedback from the field tells us that since the delivery of our first wheelchairs to Luanda in 2001, physically disabled children are attending school, adults are able to work and the quality of water, food and clothing in these people's homes has greatly improved.

Other friends, companies and organizations that have helped us over the years include:

Abbas I. Yousef Foundation

Altria Group Inc.

Behring Sons Foundation

Catherine Reynolds Foundation

Christopher Reeve Paralysis Foundation

The Greek Orthodox Church

The Hofmann Foundation

Hyundai

The Knights of Malta

Major League Baseball

Met Life

Ralph and Betty Englestad

Ronald McDonald House Charities

The Royal Family Foundation of Saudi Arabia

Samaritan's Purse

Samsung

Seaton Institute

Sister Cities International

Sisters of Charity

Smithsonian Magazine

Thomas Seeno Foundation

Wells Fargo Foundation

Some Wheelchair Foundation
International Distribution Partners — *Countries of Distribution*

1	Aasha Rotary Centre for the Handicapped	India, Bangladesh
2	Afghan Center	Afghanistan
3	Africare	Cape Verde, Algeria, Niger, Rwanda, Senegal, Somalia, Sudan, Western Sahara, Zambia
4	Aid To The Church In Russia	Russia
5	Airline Ambassadors	Bolivia
6	Al-Hussein Society	Jordan
7	American Friends of Alyn Hospital	Israel
8	American Nicaragua Foundation	Nicaragua
9	American Red Cross	Armenia
10	Amity Foundation	China
11	Archbishop of Ghana	Ghana
12	Arco Iris Hospital	Bolivia
13	Asociación Pro Desarrollo de la Persona con Discapacidad	Peru
14	Asociación de Paraplejicos	Ecuador
15	Assaf Harofeh Medical Center	Israel
16	Association for the Physically Disabled	South Africa
17	Bahamas Association For The Physically Disabled	Bahamas
18	Barbados Council for the Disabled	Barbados
19	Belize Council for the Visually Impaired	Belize
20	Puyallup Rotary Club, Washington	USA
21	Calcutta Hospital	India
22	Caritas Arquidiocesana Hospital Infantil Juan Pablo	Guatemala

23	Caritas Makeni	Sierra Leone
24	Catholic Charities	USA
25	Catholic Relief Services	Nigeria, Angola
26	Center for Independent Living of South Florida	USA
27	Centro Nacional de Rehabilitación	Mexico
28	Cheshire Home	Papua New Guinea, Ethiopia
29	ChevronTexaco	Angola
30	Child Care Trust	Nigeria
31	Children's Orthopedic Hospital #1	Guatemala
32	The Children Foundation	Puerto Rico
33	China Disabled Persons' Federation	China
34	Christ for Humanity	Guatemala
35	Christian Orthopedic Partners	Ecuador
36	The Church of Jesus Christ of Latter-day Saints	Ukraine, USA, Samoa, Japan, Korea, Malaysia, Armenia, Argentina
37	President of Colombia	Colombia
38	Comisión Nacional de Personas Discapacitadas	Argentina
39	Consejo Nacional de Discapacidades	Ecuador, Costa Rica
40	Convalescent Aid Society	USA
41	Corporacion Cristino de Ayuda al Discapacitado	Ecuador
42	Counterpart International	Belarus, Turkmenistan, Uzbekistan, Ukraine, Kyrgyzstan, Moldova, Tajikistan, Kazakhstan, Georgia
43	Croatian Union of the Physically Disabled	Croatia
44	Crossroads International	Hong Kong
45	David Behring, Princeton Class of 1977	Guatemala, Vietnam

46	Deseret Industries	Mozambique
47	Direct Relief International	Albania, Brazil, Colombia, Honduras, Peru, Ecuador, India
48	Diwaliben Mohanlal Mehta Charitable Trust	India
49	Dominican Rehabilitation Association/Entrena	Dominican Republic
50	Domov SV Karla	Czech Republic
51	Englezakis Group	South Africa
52	Ethiopian National Assoc. of Physically Handicapped	Ethiopia
53	Familias en Progreso	El Salvador
54	Filipino War Veterans Foundation (FILVETS), Inc.	Philippines
55	First Lady of Angola	Angola
56	First Lady of Argentina	Argentina
57	First Lady of Baja, Mexico	Mexico
58	First Lady of Bolivia	Bolivia
59	First Lady of Brazil	Brazil
60	First Lady of Coahuila, Mexico	Mexico
61	First Lady of Colombia	Colombia
62	First Lady of Costa Rica	Costa Rica
63	First Lady of Ecuador	Ecuador
64	First Lady of Egypt	Egypt
65	First Lady of El Salvador	El Salvador
66	First Lady of Ethiopia	Ethiopia
67	First Lady of Guatemala	Guatemala
68	First Lady of Honduras	Honduras
69	First Lady of México	Mexico
70	First Lady of Madagascar	Madagascar
71	First Lady of Nicaragua	Nicaragua
72	First Lady of Nigeria	Nigeria

73	First Lady of Panama	Panama
74	First Lady of Paraguay	Paraguay
75	First Lady of Peru	Peru
76	First Lady of Tamaulipas	Mexico
77	First Lady of Tanzania	Tanzania
78	First Lady of Uruguay	Uruguay
79	First Lady Viviane Wade	Morocco
80	Fist Lady of Chile	Chile
81	Fondacionia Liahonia	Albania
82	Fondo Nacional de la Discapacidad	Chile
83	Fondo Unido Rotario de México	Mexico
84	Food For The Poor, Inc.	Trinidad and Tobago
85	Forest Town School	South Africa
86	Foundation for the Enhancement and Enrichment of Life	Trinidad and Tobago
87	Foundation to Encourage the Potential of the Disabled	Thailand
88	Fundación Maria	Uruguay
89	Fundación Por Los Niños Del Peru	Peru
90	Fundación Pro Impedidos	Panama
91	Fundación Promoción y Desarrollo de la Mujer (PRODEMU)	Chile
92	Fundación Reina	Spain
93	GOAL "Get Out And Live"	Kenya
94	Goodwill Industries	USA
95	Guatemala Secretaria de Obras Sociales	Guatemala
96	Haifa Foundation	Israel
97	Helping Hands International	Vietnam
98	Heracles Company	Greece

99	Hope Haven International Ministry	Romania, Vietnam, Guatemala, Nicaragua, Somalia, Ukraine, Dominican Republic Mexico, Pakistan, Russia, El Salvador, Israel (Gaza), Syria, Honduras
100	Hope Worldwide	Cambodia, Philippines
101	Hospitals Without Frontiers	Belgium
102	Ikamva Labantu	South Africa
103	Instituto Nacional del Niño y la Familia (INNFA)	Ecuador
104	International Christian Committee In Israel	Israel
105	International Red Crescent Society (ICRC)	Egypt, Iran
106	International Service of Hope	Latvia
107	JAF Ministries	China
108	Kenya Programmes of Disabled Persons	Kenya
109	Kham Aid Foundation	China/Tibet
110	Knights of Malta	USA
111	Kham Aid	Tibet, Nepal
112	L.I.F.E.	India
113	Life for Relief and Development	Iraq
114	Lion's Club/Club de Leones	Peru
115	Les Enfants De La Victoire	Cape Verde
116	Liga Za Prava Vozickaru	Czech Republic
117	Major League Baseball	Mexico, Puerto Rico, USA
118	Malawi Council for the Handicapped	Malawi
119	Malaysian Leprosy Relief Association	Malaysia
120	Mark 2 Ministries	El Salvador
121	Mayor of Skopye	Macedonia
122	Medical Outreach for Armenians, Inc.	Armenia

123	Mercy Corp.	Montenegro
124	Mercy Ships	Sierra Leone
125	Mfomo Nkhambule	Swaziland
126	Ministerio de Salud Publica	Uruguay
127	Ministry of Health National Ctr. of Physical Rehabilitation	Samoa
128	Ministry of Health	Jamaica
129	Ministry of Labour and Social Affairs	Ethiopia
130	Ministry of Social Affairs	Serbia
131	Ministry of Social Welfare	Sierra Leone
132	Ministry of Women and Veteran's Affairs	Cambodia
133	Mission of Mercy	Nepal
134	Mission of Charity	Kenya
135	Christian Missions Unlimited	Brazil
136	Mobility Project	Nepal
137	North Atlantic Treaty Organization (NATO)	Estonia
138	National Council Of the Disabled Persons of Zimbabwe	Zimbabwe
139	National Federation of Disabled Person's Association	Hungary
140	National Rehabilitation Center	Laos
141	Nelson Mandela Foundation	South Africa
142	Northern Regional Center for Independent Living	USA
143	Nour Int'l Relief Aid	Jordan
144	President of Botswana	Botswana
145	President of Malta	Malta
146	President Sam Nujoma	Namibia
147	Oakland Athletics Baseball Company	Dominican Republic

148 Operation USA	Cuba
149 Pakistan Society for the Rehabilitation of the Disabled	Pakistan
150 Patient's Friends Society	Israel/Gaza
151 Perpetual Help for Africa	Nigeria
152 Prime Minister of Trinidad and Tobago	Trinidad and Tobago
153 Prince Kwame Kludjeson	Ghana
154 Princess of Thailand	Thailand
155 Project Hope	Bosnia, Kosovo, Macedonia
156 Rajkot Blood Bank	India
157 Red Cross of Bosnia/Herzegovina	Bosnia
158 Rehab Assoc. of Burundi	Burundi
159 Rehab Assoc. of Central African Republic	Central African Republic
160 Rehab Assoc. of Chad	Chad
161 Rehab Assoc. of Congo/Brazzaville	Democratic Republic of the Congo
162 Rehab Assoc. of Ecuatorial Guinea	Ecuatorial Guinea
163 Rehab Assoc. of Gabon	Gabon
164 Rehab Assoc. of Rwanda	Rwanda
165 Rehabilitation International	Dominican Republic
166 RHB Chicago	USA
167 Rotary Clubs Worldwide	South Africa, Argentina, Honduras, Nigeria, Mexico, Philippines, Turkey, Brazil, Venezuela, Sri Lanka, Kenya, Uganda, India, China, Peru, Chile, Bangladesh, Nepal, Suriname, Belize, Papua New Guinea, Bolivia, Jamaica, Israel, Panama, Malaysia, Morocco, Haiti, Dominican Republic, Trinidad and Tobago, St. Croix, Costa Rica, St. Lucia, Korea, Lebanon, El Salvador, Mozambique, Ukraine, Nicaragua, Ecuador

168	Russian Children's Fund	Russia
169	Salvadoran American Health Foundation	El Salvador
170	Samaritan's Purse	Uzbekistan, El Salvador, Eritrea
171	Sanabil Association	Lebanon
172	Scottlee Holdings	Zimbabwe
173	Seton Institute	Israel, Vietnam, Nigeria
174	Shanghai Disabled Person's Federation	China
175	Sirindhorn National Medical Rehabilitation Center	Thailand
176	St. Vincent's Center	Haiti
177	The Association For The Physically Disabled	Kenya
178	The Auto Collection/Imperial Palace Hotel	USA
179	The Haifa Foundation	Israel
180	The Jairos Jiri Association	Zimbabwe
181	The Salvation Army	USA
182	Tianjin Fund Organization For Disabled Persons	China
183	Transitions Foundation of Guatemala	Guatemala
184	Turkish Red Crescent	Turkey
185	Tzu Chi University	Taiwan
186	UNICEF	Kosovo
187	University of Guam	Guam
188	U.S. Embassy	Latvia, Afghanistan
189	Vamos México Fundación	Mexico
190	Victorian Center	Algeria
191	Wheels for Humanity	Mongolia, USA, Pakistan
192	World Vision	Zambia, Romania
193	Zaka Rescue Recovery	Israel

THE WHEELCHAIR FOUNDATION

I launched the Wheelchair Foundation in June 2000 as a 501(c)3 nonpartisan, nondenominational, nonprofit organization. Its mission is to bring hope, dignity and freedom to the estimated 100 million or more people suffering from immobility in the world. Since beginning its mission, the Foundation has grown significantly. The headquarters is in Danville, California, but we now have offices and chapters in Las Vegas, Nevada; New York City; Washington, D.C.; Ft. Lauderdale, Florida; Shanghai, China; Canada and Australia.

Here is a partial list of the people who have made our mission a success:

California Headquarters

David Behring has served as the President of the Wheelchair Foundation since 2003. Prior to that, he was the president of the Blackhawk Automotive Museum, a Smithsonian Institution affiliate that is one of the most spectacular classic automobile collections in the world. David spent five years (1993–1997) as president of the Seattle Seahawks and was a member of the NFL Finance Committee. A graduate of Princeton University and the University of Miami Law School, he spent most of his business career in home-building and development in California. David, a Rotarian, has been very active in both professional and community service organizations for almost 30 years and has served on numerous boards during this period. He is a member of the Smithsonian's National Museum of American History Board and is assisting his father on various projects of that institution.

Jeff Behring, Director of Special Events, helps to "sow the seeds" of the Foundation and its work around the world. He is also a property manager and a general contractor, building custom homes as well as semi-custom homes and commercial and warehouse buildings. He also does tenant improvement work. Jeff is a Rotarian and a Paul Harris Fellow with the Danville, California, Rotary Club. He received a Bachelor of Arts degree from Southern Methodist University in 1980, concentrating in real estate and finance. He is married and has four children.

Thomas Behring handles Africa, the Pacific Islands and Southeast Asia for the Foundation's operations department. He grew up in Florida, and attended college in California. He has lived in Blackhawk for 20 years and has worked at the Foundation for two years. Previously, he worked in construction and homebuilding until the age of 30, at the Blackhawk Classic Car Collection for four years, then at the Blackhawk Automotive Museum for 15 years.

Eva Brook, Regional Operations Manager for Latin America, joined the Wheelchair Foundation in October 2003. Eva manages all wheelchair deliveries to Latin America and the Caribbean, the Foundation's second-busiest region. Her primary focus is the efficient delivery and distribution of wheelchairs through capacity building, facilitating between donors and in-country partner organizations, relationship building and problem solving. Eva holds a Master of Law and Diplomacy from the Fletcher School at Tufts University, where she specialized in negotiation and conflict resolution and humanitarian aid. Eva speaks English, Spanish, German and French. Before joining the Wheelchair Foundation, Eva worked on CARE's human rights framework for development and mediated disputes for the Massachusetts Department of Telecommunications and Energy.

Charli Butterfield, Assistant Director of Distribution, Africa, is responsible for selecting NGOs to receive and distribute wheelchairs to those in need of mobility in Africa and other countries that Ken Behring visits with his aircraft. She also has been Ken Behring's international events coordinator for 12 years, including four years at the Foundation. She has participated in all of Ken's humanitarian efforts aboard his aircraft, including shipping educational materials and clothing to Africa, shipping wheelchairs around the world, setting up important meetings with heads of state and coordinating wheelchair distributions in the "bush country" of Africa.

Earl Callison is the Chief Financial Officer for Kenneth E. Behring Investments and the related Blackhawk entities. He is the Vice President and a member of the Board of Directors of the

Wheelchair Foundation. Earl has been with the Foundation since it began. Prior to his association with Ken Behring, Earl managed the Northern California Real Estate Division for First Interstate Bank. His banking career also included positions with Bank of America and the Federal Reserve Bank of San Francisco. Earl is a licensed California real estate broker and earned a Bachelor of Science degree in business administration from the University of California at Berkeley. He resides in Lafayette with his wife and three children.

Amanda Ferguson has worked for the Foundation for four years as an administrative assistant. Her responsibilities include depositing and recording donations, sending out cameras and placards to NGOs, creating and mailing all of the presentation folders for the donors and handling other administrative tasks.

Brandi Haley joined the Public Education Department as an assistant in February 2003. Brandi helps with donor inquiries, processing donations, and shipping and handling materials to potential donors, staff and all Foundation offices. Brandi's attention to detail is applied to creating personalized donor marketing material kits, executing the elements needed for conferences and events and participating in presenting the Foundation to the public.

Amy Harris is the Foundation's Public Education Manager. She joined the organization in 2003 to help educate people about the worldwide need for wheelchairs and the Foundation's mission through presentations and participation with service clubs, religious organizations and corporate giving campaigns. Her specialized skills are used in the print production of public education materials and direct mail.

Joel Hodge has been with the Wheelchair Foundation since 2000, working in operations, transportation, development and more. He has served as photographer, in-field video producer, scriptwriter, program director and director of operations, recently director of operations for the Eastern Hemisphere. Joel has traveled extensively throughout the world (more than 50 countries in the past four years) to some of the most depressed and poverty-stricken corners of the planet to distribute wheelchairs and to represent the Foundation. Joel has had the honor of meeting world leaders and many of the forgotten disabled who exist in every country. A graduate of Southwest Missouri State University, Joel has an extensive banking background and has worked for the Federal Reserve Bank and in private banking, as well as serving as a research and development scientist in the biotech industry. He and his wife, Molly, live in North Oakland and are expecting their first child.

Jeff Juri has been the accounting manager with Foundation for two years. His responsibilities include donor contributions and acknowledgments, preparing monthly financial statements and handling donor customer service. A graduate of San Diego State University, he has more than 20 years of experience in accounting. He is married with one son.

Jason Katz is the Associate Director of Community Relations, and is responsible for the content of the foundation's quarterly newsletter, annual report and website. He also conducts public speaking engagements to groups that are interested in the Foundation's mission. Jason is a graduate of the University of California, Davis.

Chris Lewis is Director of Public Education/Development for the Foundation and a member of its Board of Directors. When Ken

Behring owned the Seattle Seahawks, the team's foundation was the largest donor to the Muscular Dystrophy Association in Washington state. Chris's dad, Jerry Lewis, has been the national chairman of MDA since 1952 and Chris has worked on the MDA Telethon since 1972. Chris and Ken met as a result of an MDA art exhibit at the Blackhawk Museum in 1994. Chris joined the Foundation prior to its launch in 2000 and produces all print, video and electronic media to promote its mission. Chris developed the working relationship with Rotary Clubs worldwide in 2000 and is responsible for the creation of Wheelchair Foundation Canada, Australia and United Kingdom with Rotarian volunteers in each country. Chris is a member of the Rotary Club of San Ramon, California and is a Knight of Columbus.

Matt Montague is an executive assistant to Ken Behring and is the Foundation's Director of Community Relations. He travels with Ken and follows up with groups and individuals within the United States. Matt also works on the writing, editing and design of the Foundation's newsletter, annual report and website. He handles media relations with television, newspapers and other outlets, as well as oversees speaking engagements, presentations and contacts with individuals, groups, clubs and organizations to help raise funds for wheelchairs.

Laura Maria Morales joined the Wheelchair Foundation as a transportation and logistics coordinator in June 2004. Laura supports the operations team, especially with Latin American countries, as she is originally from Colombia and is fluent in Spanish. Laura handles documentation for shipments, advises in-country partners on wheelchair import and clearing processes and resolves customs issues to expedite wheelchair deliveries. Laura is certified in translation from the National University of Colombia and from the National

Hispanic University in San Jose, California. Before joining the Foundation, Laura worked as Assistant to the International Trade Director for the Ministry of Foreign Trade in Bogotá, Colombia.

Matt Newman started working as the Foundation's webmaster in September 2003. He has redesigned the Foundation's website, making it more informative, accessible, database-driven and interactive. He has also assisted with various technical projects, including multimedia presentations, DVD, CD-ROM and videocassette production, as well as database management of the organization's mailing list.

Mark Packard joined the Foundation team in early 2001 and is Associate Director of Public Education and Development. Mark works very closely with Chris Lewis in the coordination of Rotary Club and District speaking presentations and coordination of Rotarian sponsored projects around the world. Mark has developed the first cause-related marketing programs for the Foundation and is involved on a daily basis in the review of all materials and promotions being used around the world by groups, organizations and individuals in the promotion of the Foundation's mission and the raising of contributions. Mark and his wife Vera are members of the Rotary Club of San Ramon, California.

Gerry Riley is a transportation and logistics coordinator for the Foundation. After a career in computer hardware and software support, he joined the Foundation in 2003 to help get the wheelchairs manufactured and delivered. He says he experienced a "pretty steep learning curve" in the world of ocean freight. His earlier skill set did come in handy, though—he was able to pull together disparate functions and data, and to automate much of the shipping process. He enjoys working at an organization for which the object isn't to make "tons of money," but rather to give something to those in need.

Angie Shen is the latest member of our team in California. After graduating from Saint Mary's College in California with degrees in finance and economics, she worked in the private sector. At the Foundation, she is an executive assistant to Ken Behring, accompanying him on many of his trips around the world. A native of China, she has been especially involved in wheelchair distributions and business there. She calls her experience with the Foundation "a truly unique and exciting journey."

Vladimir Todorovic is a regional operations manager who has been with the Wheelchair Foundation since October 2003. Prior to this post, Vladimir worked as a business consultant and a microfinance program manager for the United Nations. Vladimir's primary responsibility is Eastern Europe, with a particular focus on Russia, where he helped the Foundation overcome language and customs barriers and increase wheelchair delivery severalfold. Vladimir holds a Master of Arts degree in international development and negotiations from the Fletcher School of Law and Diplomacy at Tufts University. He speaks Serbian/Bosnian/Croatian, Russian and Italian.

Annette Vineyard is an executive assistant to Ken Behring and is Regional Operations Director for the Middle East. After working for the Behrings as a household manager and assistant, she joined the Foundation when it launched in 2000. Her experience as a distribution, warehouse and quality control manager for an industrial company helped prepare her for her work at the Foundation, where those functions are important to operations and deliveries. She has been on dozens of wheelchair distributions, calling them a "wonderful thing, an instant life-changing experience" for both the recipient and the team member. She has been joined on distributions by her daughter, Tara, who works part-time on Foundation donor relations.

Marsha Warner, CPA, is the Foundation's controller. She started working with the Foundation in September 2001. She works closely with auditors to set up policies and procedures in accounting. She worked for nine years in public accounting for a local firm in Fremont, California, and 12 years in the construction and insurance industries as a controller. She is married with two children.

Lee Winter, Assistant to the President, has been employed with Behring entities since 1984 as contracts administrator during land development, property manager of Blackhawk Plaza and the Blackhawk Commercial Owner's Association upon completion of the commercial center and administrator of Blackhawk Automotive Museum. When David Behring assumed the role of President of the Wheelchair Foundation, he asked Lee to serve as his assistant to work on special projects, research, fundraising and community events, donor relations, organizational and communications issues and community outreach. A graduate of the University of Michigan, Lee has a Bachelor of Science degree in elementary education and she holds a lifetime California teaching credential. Lee is active in the community and currently serves on the Danville Area Chamber of Commerce Board Executive Committee as Vice Chair of Promotions.

China Office

Lynn Shaw joined the Foundation's China office as an assistant in 2004. Her responsibilities include purchase order operation, wheelchair delivery, photo collection, office logistic work and assisting her colleagues. She says she tries her best with each job to ensure that wheelchairs are sent to the neediest recipients. She earned a Bachelor of Arts in international trade English from China Hunan Normal University in 2003. Before joining the Foundation, she worked as an administrative assistant and assistant to a marketing manager at a computer software company.

Jing Sun is an executive assistant to Ken Behring and Director for Chinese Affairs for the China office. She earned a Bachelor of Arts degree in foreign languages from Dalian University and a Master of Business Administration from the University of Leeds, Leeds, United Kingdom. She was the first employee of the Foundation's China office when it opened in March 2002. She is responsible for the business development, operation and management of the office. She travels on distributions and also travels frequently between the United States and China for various projects. She calls helping people and working with Ken Behring "the experience of a lifetime."

Katherine Yan joined the China office as a project manager in 2003. Her major responsibilities include processing purchase orders, setting up distribution ceremonies, overseeing quality control and maintaining the Foundation's relationship with the government. She received a Bachelor of Arts degree in English language and literature from Dalian University. She worked for three years for a major shipping company in logistics, customer service and sales. After that, she spent a year in England and earned a Master's Degree in international marketing management from the University of Leeds. She says she enjoys her job because it enables her to help others, especially the neediest.

Ling Yan joined the China office as Public Relations Manager in 2004. Her work focuses on development and implementation of public relations campaigns and fundraising activities. She is also responsible for media relations, sponsor relations and volunteer programs. Born in Shanghai, she received a Bachelor of Arts degree in communications from Shanghai International Studies University. She has experience as a part-time radio program presenter and project manager of the China Shanghai International Arts Festival. Before joining the Foundation, she worked for Shell and Fleishman-Hillard International. She says she enjoys her job because it gives her purpose in life.

Florida Office

Jack Drury met Ken Behring in August 1960 when he moved to Ft. Lauderdale, Florida. Ken was a builder, and the Drury family needed a home. The purchase of the home led to Ken Behring hiring Jack's advertising firm to handle marketing for Behring Properties. When Ken moved to California, Jack stayed in Florida. In July 2000, Jack, who was retired, called to congratulate Ken on creating the Wheelchair Foundation. Ken wanted to take advantage of Jack's talents, and a month later, he opened the Southeast Office of the Wheelchair Foundation in Ft. Lauderdale. He oversees Wheelchair Foundation activities in the southeastern United States, South and Central America and the Caribbean.

Nevada Office

Don Williams, President of the Nevada chapter, oversees wheelchair distributions in Nevada as a friend and volunteer of the Foundation. The Nevada chapter has distributed more than 2,000 wheelchairs in the state. Through his friendship with the late Nevada businessman Ralph Englestad, who was a native of North Dakota, the chapter also has distributed 2,100 wheelchairs in that state. Don's full-time work is buying and selling classic cars; he is the world's leading expert on prewar classics. But he fell in love with what Ken Behring is doing around the world and has tried to help the Foundation in any way he can, including raising more than $1 million for it.

New York Office

Wilson Kimball serves as Executive Director of the Wheelchair Foundation's New York state office. Wilson is the former Chief-of-Staff and Counsel to First Lady Libby Pataki of New York state. During her nine years in the Governor's Office, Wilson worked extensively on Mrs. Pataki's agenda, including health care and literacy issues. She also worked closely with the Governor's Community Affairs Department. Through her daily contact with New York's ethnic communities, Wilson developed a strong multicultural network. Wilson is a 1990 honors graduate of Skidmore College, with a degree in political science. She also holds a J.D. from Fordham University School of Law. Married to Murad Raheem, Wilson spends her free time writing.

Elizabeth "Libby" Pataki, a consultant to the Foundation, has served as first lady of New York state since her husband, Governor George E. Pataki, took office in 1995. An advocate for health issues, Mrs. Pataki has been on the forefront in the fight against domestic violence, breast cancer and heart disease. She has also served as spokesperson for Child Health Plus and Family Health Plus. A life-long devotee of public service, Mrs. Pataki is the daughter of an American diplomat father and French-Moroccan mother. As a result of her father's career, the first lady lived all over the world before settling in New York. The mother of four children, Mrs. Pataki is continually inspired by the work of her husband in the aftermath of September 11th and by the endless spirit and selfless enthusiasm of Ken Behring.

Washington, D.C., Office

Cheryl Shaw Barnes is a Co-Executive Director of the Foundation's Washington, D.C., office. A noted children's book author, illustrator and publisher, Cheryl began volunteering with the Foundation in 2002. Ken Behring asked her to join the organization in 2003. She is a liaison for the Foundation with the U.S. Department of State and U.S. Department of Defense. She also oversees congressional relations for the organization. She is a member of the Rotary Club of Washington, D.C.

Peter Barnes is a Co-Executive Director of the Foundation's office in Washington, D.C. A former journalist and broadcaster, he works with his wife, Cheryl, and assists the Foundation in public relations, congressional relations and fundraising.

Canada Office

Christiana Flessner has been Executive Director of the Wheelchair Foundation Canada since January 2003. She has taken part in wheelchair distributions in Mexico, Papua New Guinea, Washington and California and draws from those experiences during speaking presentations, many of them to Rotarians across Canada. Christiana grew up in a tiny village in northern Germany. She received a Bachelor of Arts in Economics from the University of British Columbia/Vancouver in 1979. Over the years, in addition to helping run the family business in land development and property management and raising four children, Christiana has always been very involved in the local community. She became a Rotarian in 2001 and heard about the work of the Wheelchair Foundation at her first District Assembly. Coming from a rural community, she has always treasured personal relationships and the practical approach to solving problems and found a way to combine the two by being involved in both organizations.

WHEELCHAIR FOUNDATION OFFICES

Wheelchair Foundation World Headquarters
President – David Behring
3700 Blackhawk Plaza Circle
Danville, CA 94506 USA
Telephone: (877) 378-3839 Toll Free
(925) 791-2340
Fax: (925) 791-2346
E-mail: info@wheelchairfoundation.org

Nevada Office
Chapter President – Donald E. Williams
Director – John Williams
Imperial Palace Hotel & Casino
3535 Las Vegas Boulevard South, 5th Floor
Las Vegas, NV 89109 USA
Telephone: (800) 851-3706 Toll Free
(702) 794-3180
Fax: (702) 794-3392
E-mail: comments@wheelchairsfornevada.org

New York Office
Executive Director – Wilson Kimball
245 Park Avenue, 39th Floor, Suite 97
New York, NY 10167 USA
Telephone: (212) 792-4265
Fax: (212) 692-0401

Southeast Office
President – Jack Drury
(Member – Rotary Club of Ft. Lauderdale)
2800 East Commercial Boulevard, Suite 207
Fort Lauderdale, FL 33308 USA
Telephone: (877) 378-3839 Toll Free
(954) 776-0722
Fax: (954) 776-1290
E-mail: jdrury@wheelchairfoundation.org

Washington, D.C., Office
Co-Executive Directors – Peter and Cheryl Barnes
P.O. Box 17083
Alexandria, VA 22302 USA
Telephone: (703) 684-9820
Fax: (703) 684-7955
E-mail: cbarnes@wheelchairfoundation.org

China Office
Katherine Yan
27th Floor, Building A, Far East International Plaza
319 Xian Xia Road, Changning Area 200051
Shanghai, P. R. China
Telephone:
+86 21 6235 1675
+86 21 6235 1446
Fax: +86 21 6235 1609
E-mail: kyan@wheelchairfoundation.org

Wheelchair Foundation Australia
Executive Director – Harry Melkonian
P.O. Box 234
Gosford, NSW 2250
Australia
Telephone: 13 0076 0581
Fax: 02 4323 1019
E-mail: hmelkonian@wheelchairfoundation.org.au
Website: http://wheelchairfoundation.org.au

Wheelchair Foundation Canada
La Fondation de Chaise Roulante Canada
Executive Director – Christiana Flessner
P.O. Box 75038
White Rock, B.C. V4B 5L3
Canada
Telephone: 866-666-2411 (Toll Free within Canada)
(604) 536-2022
Fax: (604) 536-9831
E-mail: cflessner@wheelchairfoundation.ca
Website: http://wheelchairfoundation.ca

Appendix C
HELPING THE WHEELCHAIR FOUNDATION

Wheelchair Foundation Donation Form

Tens of millions of people in the world are in need of a wheelchair and cannot afford one. These are children, teens and adults who lack mobility because of disease, accident, war or advanced age. With a wheelchair, they will have their lives instantly changed; they will be able to go to school, work, worship, or just outside for the first time in years or ever. For them, a wheelchair means hope, mobility and freedom.

The Wheelchair Foundation delivers wheelchairs worldwide by 280-wheelchair containers from suppliers in China at a rate of more than 10,000 per month. Because of this volume, we are able to deliver a wheelchair that would sell for approximately $500 in the United States for an average of $150 each. We have been gifted funds to combine with each new $75 donation to deliver each wheelchair, until these combinable gifted funds have been exhausted.

The Wheelchair Foundation distributes wheelchairs in a country of destination with approved distribution partners. They identify the recipients and then propertly seat them in their new wheelchairs. Donors will be invited to choose the country or region of the wheelchairs' destination from a list of countries with which the Foundation enjoys established and successful distribution relationships.

Please copy this two-page form and fill out donor information completely.

_____ $75 _____ $150 _____ Other $_____

Donor/Contact Name _____

Address _____

_____

_____

City _____ State/Province _____ ZIP _____

Country_____

Phone _____ Fax _____

E-mail _____

Wording on Presentation Folder
(See example on www.wheelchairfoundation.org)
"The Wheelchair Foundation wishes to thank..."

___ Rotary Club (above) ___ Donor (above) ___ Other (see below)

For the gift made _____ No designation requested _____

In Honor of: _____

In Memory of:_____

I (we) would like to see the wheelchairs delivered to:

_____

Any country in need _____
Check Enclosed _____
Credit Card:
_____ Visa _____ MasterCard _____ American Express ___Discover

Name as it appears on card _____

Card Number _____

Exp. Date _____

Signature _____

Please make checks payable to:
The Wheelchair Foundation
3820 Blackhawk Road
Danville, California 94506
USA

Credit card form can be mailed to address above.

Toll Free: (877) 378-3839
(925) 736-8234
Fax: (925) 791-2346
www.wheelchairfoundation.org
E-mail: info@wheelchairfoundation.org

The Wheelchair Foundation distributes wheelchairs through an established network of nongovernmental and other organizations that are certified to import humanitarian aid duty free, take full responsibility for the importation, transportation and proper distribution of the wheelchairs, and then return photographs to us of each wheelchair recipient, using the numbered placards and single-use cameras that we supply. The photographs are then used to create the presentation folders that are sent to Wheelchair Foundation donors.

If all of the criteria listed above are met by an organization in a specific country, then the country is considered by the Wheelchair Foundation to be one with an established and successful distribution relationship. Absolutely no political, ethnic or religious affiliations are considered when evaluating any region of the world for the distribution of wheelchairs. Since the establishment of the Wheelchair Foundation on June 13, 2000, we have continually worked to develop successful distribution relationships in as many countries as possible. During this learning process, we have been forced to remove some countries from the list, but continue to work for new or better relationships that will allow us to serve more parts of the world under our established program.

The Wheelchair Foundation enjoys established and successful distribution relationships in the countries listed below. This list will be constantly modified as we work to expand our distribution network. In some cases, countries may be removed from the list due to distribution difficulties. Please confirm distribution ability with Chris Lewis, Director of Public Education at the Wheelchair Foundation by e-mail: clewis@wheelchairfoundation.org.

East Asia
China/Tibet
Japan
South Korea

Northern Asia
Mongolia

North America
Canada
United States

Southern Asia
Afghanistan
Bangladesh
Nepal
Pakistan
Sri Lanka

Southwest Asia
Armenia
Georgia
Turkey

Oceania
French Polynesia
Micronesia
Samoa
Tonga

Middle East
Cyprus
Iran
Iraq
Israel
Jordan
Lebanon
Palestinians/Israel

Central Asia
Kazakhstan
Kyrgyzstan
Tajikistan
Turkmenistan
Uzbekistan

Southeast Asia
Cambodia
Indonesia
Laos
Malaysia
Papua New Guinea
Philippines
Thailand
Vietnam

Central America
Belize
Costa Rica
El Salvador
Guatemala
Honduras
Mexico

Caribbean
Bahamas
Cuba
Dominican Republic
Haiti
Jamaica
Saint Lucia (U.K.)

South America
Argentina
Bolivia
Chile
Colombia
Ecuador
Paraguay
Nicaragua
Panama
Trinidad and Tobago
Virgin Islands (U.S.)
Peru
Suriname
Uruguay
Venezuela

Eastern Europe
Albania
Belarus
Bosnia-Herzegovina
Bulgaria
Croatia
Estonia
Kosovo
Latvia
Lithuania
Macedonia
Moldova
Montenegro
Poland
Romania
Ukraine
Yugoslavia

Africa
Algeria
Angola
Botswana
Cape Verde
Egypt
Eritrea
Ethiopia
Ghana
Kenya
Madagascar
Mozambique
Uganda
Rwanda
Sierra Leone
South Africa
Tanzania
Zimbabwe

For more information, to see an updated list of destination countries, to watch videos of wheelchair distributions around the world or to donate online, please visit:

www.wheelchairfoundation.org

For multiple donations, please send all Presentation Folders to:

Name _____

Address _____

City _____

State/Province _____ ZIP _____

Country_____

Gift made in the name of (optional):

_____

_____

_____

_____

_____

_____

_____

_____

Appendix D
OUR INTERNATIONAL BOARD OF ADVISORS

These are the people who have provided direction and assistance in our travels and deliveries throughout the world. Their help has been invaluable.

King Juan Carlos and Queen Sofia of Spain Co-Chairs

Prince Alexander and **Princess Katherine** of Yugoslavia
Carl A. Anderson, Supreme Knight, Knights of Columbus
Robert M. Berdahl, Chancellor, University of California
     at Berkeley
Wendy W. de Berger, First Lady of Guatemala
Ruth Correa Leite Cardoso, Ph.D., Former First Lady of Brazil
Lorena Clare Facio De Rodriguez Echeverria, Former First
     Lady of Costa Rica
Joel Ehrenkranz, Ehrenkranz & Ehrenkranz, New York
Professor Sir Harry Fang, M.D., Chairman, Council
     for Physically & Mentally Disabled, Hong Kong
Mary Flake De Flores, First Lady of Honduras
Lourdes Rodriguez De Flores, First Lady of El Salvador
Whitey Ford, Baseball Hall of Fame

Martha Sahagun Fox, First Lady of Mexico
Imants Freibergs, First Gentleman of Latvia
Valery Giscard D'Estaing, Former President of France
Mikhail Gorbachev, Former President of the USSR
Doug Heir, President of the National Spinal Cord Injury
    Association
Kenneth Hofmann, Oakland Athletics Baseball Team
Tim Honey, Executive Director, Sister Cities International
Michael A. Jacobs, Chairman, Discovery International
    Associates, Inc.
Jack Kemp, Former U.S. Representative and Secretary of Housing
    and Urban Development
Mrs. Andree Lahoud, First Lady of Lebanon
Jerry Lewis, Entertainer/Humanitarian
Susana Galli De Gonzalez Macchi, First Lady of Paraguay
Graca Machel, Former First Lady of Mozambique/
    Mrs. Nelson Mandela
Nelson Mandela, Former President of South Africa
Ed McMahon, Radio and Television Personality
Anna Mkapa, First Lady of Tanzania
Mireya Moscoso, President of Panama
Wayne Newton, Entertainer, Las Vegas, Nevada
Maria Isabel Baquerizo De Noboa, Former First Lady
    of Ecuador
Samuel Nujoma, President of Namibia
Stella Obasanjo, First Lady of Nigeria
Dean Ornish, M.D., President and Director, Preventive Medicine
    Research Institute, University of California, San Francisco
Jack Palladino, Palladino & Sutherland, San Francisco
Arnold Palmer, Professional Golfer/Business Executive
Libby Pataki, First Lady of the State of New York
Deng Pufang, Chairman, China Disabled Persons' Federation

Virginia Gillum De Quiroga, Former First Lady of Bolivia
Prince Raad & Princess Majda Raad of Jordan
General Joseph W. Ralston, United States Air Force-Ret.
Fidel Ramos, Former President of the Philippines
Catherine B. Reynolds, American Academy of Achievement/
    CEO of Educap Inc.
Stefano Ricci, Clothing Designer
Nancy Rivard, Executive Director, Airline Ambassadors
Anna Eleanor Roosevelt, Co-Chair – Franklin & Eleanor
    Roosevelt Institute, New York
Christopher J. Rosa, PH.D., Director, Services for Students
    with Disabilities, Queens College, Flushing, New York
Yoshiaki Sakura, Chairman, Kosaido, Japan
Ana Paula Dos Santos, First Lady of Angola
Don Shula, NFL Coach/Entrepreneur
Lawrence Small, Secretary, Smithsonian Institution
Rt. Hon. Sir Michael Somare, Prime Minister,
    Papua New Guinea
Catherine Stevens, Alaska and Washington, D.C.
Viviane Wade, First Lady of Senegal
Abbas I. Yousef, ASI Agricultural Services & Investments

Honorary Members
Joe Baca, U.S. Representative, R-California
Max Cleland, Former U. S. Senator, D-Georgia
Anna G. Eshoo, U.S. Representative, D-California
Dianne Feinstein, U.S. Senator, D-California
William H. Frist, U.S. Senator, R-Tennessee
Benjamin A. Gilman, Former U.S. Representative
Daniel Inouye, U.S. Senator, D-Hawaii
Ken Lancaster, State Representative, R-Alaska
James R. Langevin, U.S. Representative, D-Rhode Island

Steve Largent, Former U.S. Representative, R-Oklahoma
Nancy Pelosi, U.S. Representative, D-California
Ted Stevens, U.S. Senator, R-Alaska
Ellen Tauscher, U.S. Representative, D-California
Tom Torlakson, State Senator, D-California